Yogavāsiṣṭha Saṅgraha

Original Sanskrit Text with Roman Transliteration, Word-meanings and English Translation of Vālmīki Yogavāsiṣṭha

Nirvāṇa Prakaraṇa (Uttarārdha)
Chapter 11

By
Dr. Ravi Prakash Arya

AMAZON BOOKS, USA
in association with
INDIAN FOUNDATION FOR VEDIC SCIENCE
1051, Sector-1, Rohtak, Haryana, India Ph. 01262-292580
Delhi Contact Ph. Nos.: 011-65188114; 09313033917
Emails: vedicscience@rediffmail.com
vedicscience@hotmail.com
Website : www.vedascience.com

First Edition

Christian era: 2015
Vikram era: 2072
Kali era: 5116
Kalpa Era: 1972949116
Brahma Era: 155521972949116

ISBN No. 81-87710-83-7

PREFACE

Yogavāsiṣṭha is a very bulky size famous book on Indian philosophy. It is known by several names, e.g. *Mahārāmāyaṇa, Ārṣarāmāyaṇa, Vasiṣṭharāmāyaṇa, Jñānavāsiṣṭha* or *Vāsiṣṭha.* This work has six chapters known as Prakaraṇas. They may be enumerated as under :

1. *Vairāgya Prakaraṇa*-This describes disillusionment with world. The issue discussed here is whether jñāna (enlightenment) or karma (willful action) is more important in attaining liberation. The answer is that both are equally important, just as a bird needs both wings to fly.

2. *Mumukṣu Vyvahāra Prakaraṇa*- This describes the qualities of a true seeker and his mental attitude.

3. *Utpatti Prakaraṇa*- This describes as to how the world was created and how it evolved.

4. *Sthiti Prakaraṇa*- This describes how the world is sustained.

5. *Upaśama Prakaraṇa*-This describes how the mind is quietened through proper understanding.

6. *Nirvāṇa Prakaraṇa*- This is about liberation. It suggests that realization of Brahma is the best way to liberation.

Nirvāṇa prakaraṇa is further divided into two parts Purvārdha (first half) and Uttarārdha (second half). It is as large as first five combined.

As per description of *Yogavāsiṣṭha*, this work contains 32,000 ślokas.

mokṣopāyābhidhāneyaṁ saṁhitā sārasṁmitā

triṁśat dve ca sahasrāṇī Jñātā nirvāṇa-dāyini. (2.17.6)

But the manuscript of *Yogavāsiṣṭha* preserved in the India Office library of London contains 28660 *ślokas*. The *Yogavāsiṣṭha* published from Nirṇaya Sāgar press Bombay contains 27687 *ślokas*. Though several other manuscripts are available, but all of them are incomplete and fragmentary. Form time to time, scholars have been producing the *Yogavāsiṣṭha* in fragments as per their interests and objectives. Today *Yogavāsiṣṭha* is available in the market in the following pocket size editions, e.g.

Laghu Yogavāsiṣṭha

Yogavāsiṣṭha śloka

Yogavāsiṣṭha sāra

Vāsiṣṭha sāra

Jñanavāsiṣṭha samuccaya etc.

We come across several commentaries on *Yogavāsiṣṭha*. Advayāraṇya son of Narahari attempted his commentary on the *Yogavāsiṣṭha* in the name of *Vāsiṣṭha Rāmāyaṇā*. In nineteenth century, Ānanda Bodhendra Sarasvatī, the disciple of Gaṅgādharendra wrote his *Tātparaya Ṭikā* on *Yogavāsiṣṭha*. Gaṅgādharendra wrote two *Bhāṣyas* on it. Mādhava Sarasvatī attempted *Pada Candrikā* commentary on this work.

Yogavāsiṣṭha is composed of several *Upākhyānas* which mainly contributed to its vast size. There are 53 important *Upākhyānas* in this work. They are as under:

1. The story of *Yogavāsiṣṭha*
2. The conversation between Rāma and Vasiṣṭha.
3. The story of Śuka
4. Vasiṣṭha's story of Origin and acquisition of knowledge.
5. The story of *Ākāśaja*
6. The story of Līlā.

7. The story of Karkaṭī Rākṣasī.
8. The story of the sons of Indu Brāhmaṇa.
9. The story of Ahalyā and Indra.
10. The story of *Citta.*
11. The story of Bala.
12. The story of *Indrajāla.*
13. *The story of Śukra.*
14. The story of Dāma, Vyāla and Kaṭa.
15. The story of Bhīma, Bhāsa and Dṛḍha.
16. The story of Daśūra.
17. Kacgītā.
18. The story of Janaka's attaining Jivanmukti.
19. The story of Puṇya and Pāvana.
20. The story of Bali.
21. The story of Prahalāda.
22. The story of Gādhī
23. The story of Uddālaka
24. The story of Suraghu
25. The story of Vītahavya
26. The story of Kāk Bhuśuṇḍa
27. The story of Queen Cuḍālā and Śikhidhvaja
28. The story of Iśvara
29. The story of Arjuna
30. The story of Śatarudra.
31. The story of Vetāla
32. The story of Bhāgīratha
33. The story of Rānī Cūḍālā

34. The story of Kirāta
35. The story of Maṇikāc
36. The story of Hastika
37. The story of Kaca
38. The story of lkṣvāku
39. The story of A Muni Settled In Turyāvasthā
40. The story of Vidyādhara
41. The story of Indra
42. The story of Maṅkī
43. The story of Manohariṇa
44. The story of Paṣāṇa
45. The story of Vipaścit
46. The story of Vaṭadhānā princes
47. The story of Śava
48. The story of Śilā
49. The story of Brahmāṇḍa
50. The story of Aindava
51. The story of Bilva
52. The story of Tāpasa
53. Kāṣṭhavaivadhika

Yogavāsiṣṭha, in fact, is the compilation of discourses delivered by the great sage Vasiṣṭha to Ram at the time of his coronation on the throne of Ayodhyā. Taking this opportunity of historic occasion, Vasiṣṭha, as per tradition, delivered his sermons on varied topics dealing with spirituality, origin of cosmos and human beings, attainment of *Mokṣa* through *Yoga* and *Samādhī*. The present treatise is bulkier in size and shape than *Rāmāyaṇa*. It sheds an ample good light on the time period of Rāma, social customs and Vedic rituals prevalent by then. It also helps unravel the mysteries of creation, decreation and *Avatāras*. It helps in ascertaining the geographical limits, i.e. longitudes and latitudes of various places during that period. Vālmīki is the author of this earliest great work on *Yoga*.

Monier Williams in his work on Indian wisdom (P.370) took notice of this work as under:

> "There is a remarkable work called *Vāsiṣṭha Rāmāyaṇa* or *Yoga Vāsiṣṭha* or *Vāsiṣṭha Mahārāmāyaṇa* in the form of an exhortation, with illustrative narratives addressed by Vasiṣṭha to his pupil, the youthful Rāma, on the best means of attaining true happiness, and considered to have been composed as an appendage to the *Rāmāyaṇa* by Vālmīki himself. There is another work of the same nature called the *Adhyātma Rāmāyaṇa* which is attributed to Vyāsa and treat of the moral and theological subjects connected with the life and acts of the great hero of Indian history. Many other works are extanṭ in the vernacular dialects having the same theme for their subjects which it is needless to notice in this place".

Vasiṣṭha known as the wisest of sages, puts forth in the first part the great question of the vanity of the world, which is shown synthetically to a great length from the state of all living existences, the instinct, inclinations and passions of men, the nature of their aims and objects, with some discussions about destiny, necessity, activity and the state of the Ātmā and Paramātmā. The second part embraces various directions for the union of the Ātmā with Paramātmā, the subjective, the objective truth and the common topics of *Yoga* philosophy.

Philosophy of Yogavāsiṣṭha

Philosophy of *Yogavāsiṣṭha* pertains to Tretā yuga. It talks about Paramātmā which is self luminous and everlasting, omnipresent and supereminent.

आत्माप्रकाशरूपो हि नित्यः सर्वगतो विभुः । 6/1.29.64

Second element discussed in detail is citta. Citta embodied Ātmā overpowered by manas. It may also be known as manas based awareness. It is deceptive and individuated element. It pertains to heart.

चित्तं शठमहंकारं विद्धिहार्दं बृहत्तमः । 6 / 1.29.64

Manas is also described like demon who has taken possession of the empty house of the body and has like an evil spirit, silenced and overpowered upon intangible citta in it.

पिशाचोऽपि मनो राम शून्यदेहगृहे स्थितः
भावयत्येष दुष्टात्मा मौनमुत्तम संस्पृशन् ।। 6 / 1.29.66

Third element discussed is the corporeal body formed of five physical elements of *Prakṛti.* In fact, this physical body is the basis or dwelling place of Ātmā often overpowered by the demon of mind. This dwelling of the body, according to *Yogavāsiṣṭha*, has the bones for its posts and the blood and flesh for its mortar and the nine holes for many windows. At the question as to who formed this body, *Yogavāsiṣṭha* replies that no one forms this body.[=]

अस्थिस्थूणं नवद्वारं रत्तफमांसावलेपनम् ।
शरीरसदनं राम न केनचिदिदं कृतम् ।। 6 / 1.28.12

But it is the manifestation of our willed decision.

संकल्पनिर्माणदेहा सहस्रशः ।

So long as we wish to live, we are dragged into corporeal body. If we cease to long for life, our emancipation becomes easy.

What is Manas ?

This question has often vexed the scholiasts and psychologists. While discussing the subject of the origin of the human body and citta (Chapter 91), the thinking power or conscious mind has been perceived in *Yogavāsiṣṭha* as the cause of all things in course of time, and the source of all its pleasurable and painful feelings, which develop and diminish in itself and never grow without it.

अविनाभाविनीनित्यं काल कांक्षिक्रमे तथा ।
सर्वमुत्पादयत्येतच्चित्तकः संविदात्मकः ।। 5.91.51

At the same time concept of sensation and citta has also been defined as the union of the breath of life with the organs and if this union is united with desire, origin of citta takes place.

यथा प्राणेन्द्रियानन्दमानन्दपवनावुभौ ।
चित्तस्योत्पादिके सार्धं यदैत वासने तदा ।। 5.91.52

This is why the living and sensitive plants which are devoid of desire are devoid of citta also.

In this course, it may be stated that end of desire, is the end of citta and end of citta tantamount to the end of birth-death cycle which is known in philosophical terms emancipation.

Difference between Citta and Sensations

The union of breath and the organs that produce sensation. But when sense organs are united with desire, they produce citta. This way living and sensitive plants or living beings which are devoid of desire are also devoid of citta or *manomayakoṣa.*

यथा प्राणेन्द्रियानन्दमानन्दपवनावुभौ ।
चित्तस्योत्पादिके सार्धं यदैते वासने तदा ।। 5.91.52

Relationship of thought and vital air

Yogavāsiṣṭha establishes keen relationship between thought and vital air. Accordingly:

संशान्ते पवनस्पन्दे यथा पांसुर्नभस्तले ।
यः प्राणपवनस्पन्दश्चित्तस्पन्दः स एव हि ।। 5.92.31

As the flying dust is set on the ground, after the gust of the wind is over, so flying thoughts of the wind are stopped, when our breathings are put to rest.

In fact there is ultimate connection between thought and vital air. The author of *Yogavāsiṣṭha* says, 'Thought commences and corresponds with vital respiration. A long thought draws a long breath and a quick one is attended with a rapid vibration of breath".

Reflection on customs

The study of *Yogavāsiṣṭha* gives sometimes an interesting insight into the old customs. Today we think that the custom of shaking hands both on meeting and parting is conspicuous to modern days and especially seem to have been borrowed from westerns. But *Yogavāsiṣṭha* tells us that this was an age old custom prevalent in the country. The following reference of *Yogavāsiṣṭha* is worth noting in this regard :

व्योम्नि योजनामात्रां तु मदनुव्रज्यया गतः।
करं करेणावष्टभ्य बलात्संरोधिः खगः।। 6 / 1.27.14

'That is the Khaga (Kāka) followed me a few miles (*yojana*) in the air, when I compelled him to return after shaking hands'.

Prohibition of idol worship

On the question of worship of the Paramātmā, the *Yogavāsiṣṭha* is very much clear. According to it, Paramātmā is of the nature of Jñāna.

आत्मसंवित्तिरूपम् – 6 / 1.29.129

So, the worship of Paramātmā can be done through accumulation of Jñāna and by forsaking the adoration of idols. Those that are devoted to any form of fictitious cult or idol worship, are subject to endless misery.

आत्मसंवित्तिरूपं तु त्यक्त्वा देवार्चनं जनाः।
कृत्रिमार्चासु ये सक्ताश्चिरं क्लेशं भजन्ति ते।। 6 / 1.29.129

In fact the idol worshippers have been compared with little children playing with their dolls.

बालक्रीडोपमं च ते अध्यात्मध्यानादृते ब्रह्मकुर्वन्तो
देवपूजनम्। 6 / 1.29.130

On the question of as to what is the best method of the worship of Brahma, the treatise further maintains that Brahma should be worshipped by accumulation of knowledge.

ज्ञानार्जनेनाविरतं पूजनीयः स सर्वदा – 6 / 1.29.131

True *pūjā* is considered to be the meditation of pure

Paramātmā (Brahma) and not otherwise, since the Brahma is the intelligent and everlasting.

त्वमेतच्चेतनाकाशमात्मानं जीवमव्ययम्।
स्वभावं विद्धि न त्वन्यः पूज्यः पूजात्मपूजनम्।। 6/1.29.132

Paramātmā is not to be worshipped with the help of external means like flowers and frankincense.

अबहिः साधनासाध्यम् – 30.31

Yogavāsiṣṭha also discards the concept of worship of mere natural and use of flowers and incense sticks in worship.

नातिदेवार्चने योग्यः पुष्पधूपचयो महान्। 6/1.30.4

Yogavāsiṣṭha, describes the act of idol worship as unlearned, simple as those of children and childish.

अव्युत्पन्नधियो ये हि बालपेलवचेतसः।
कृत्रिमार्चामयं तेषां देवार्चनमुदाहृत्तम्।। 6/1.30.5

In fact, it is due only to lack of understanding that a person worships with flowers, etc. and attribute the Paramātmā to false images of their own making.

शमवोधद्यभावे हि पुष्पाद्यैर्वार्चयन्ति हि।
मिथ्यैव कल्पितैरेतमाकारे कल्पितात्मके।। 6/1.30.6

Yogavāsiṣṭha unleashes scathing attacks on idols as to how the idols may be called as gods, who having their hands and feet, are yet devoid of their consciousness which is the pith of body.

पादपाण्यादिमानन्यो यो वा देवः प्रकल्प्यते।
संविन्मात्रादृते ब्रह्मन्किसार किल कथ्यताम्।। 6/1.30.19

Mysteries of creation

Several mysteries of creation have been unfolded in the *Yogavāsiṣṭha*. *Yogavāsiṣṭha* also unravels the secrets of creation. While shedding light on the nature of internal and external relations, it says that Brahmā took the period of one *Mahākalpa* to create this universe.

महाकल्प समाधान चिरकल्पित कल्पनम्।

वन्द्य संसक्तिवशतो ब्राह्मं स्फुरति वै वपुः।।

Thus according to *Yogavāsiṣṭha*, the whole creation accomplished not in seconds, but it took the period of महाकल्प for its completion.

Mystery of *Kūrmāvatāra*

Yogavāsiṣṭha while giving an account of past ages clarifies that *Kūrmāvatāra* is the resurrection of earth from waters and accordingly, the earth has sunk into water five times and lifted up as many times by the divine *Kūrmāvatāra* of Viṣṇu from below the overflowing ocean.

अन्तर्धानगता धात्री वारपंचकमुद्धता।
मुने पंचसु सर्गेषु कूर्मेणैव पयोनिधेः।। 6/1.22.1.2

Definition of *Manvantara*

While relating to the account of past ages, *Yogavāsiṣṭha* goes to define *Manvantara* as the measurement of time. Accordingly, *Manvantara* is a symbol of reversal of the course of world. With every *Manvantara* in fray, reversal of the course of the world takes place.

प्रतिमन्वन्तरं ब्रह्मन्विपर्यस्ते जगत्क्रमे।
संनिवेशेऽन्यथा जाते प्रयाते संश्रुते जने।। 6/1.22.37

In the process of reversal, the polarity of *Meru* is changed, the points of compass are altered, the difference in the sides of quarters takes place and so nothing remains as positive truth except our conception of it.

संस्थानमन्यथा तस्मिन्स्थिते यान्ति दिशोऽन्यथा।
न सन्नासज्जगन्मन्ये भ्रमयन्केवलं धियः।। 6/1.22.47

In the preceding lines it has been laid down that during the process of this type of reversal in a *Manvantara* north goes to other side and Meru also shifts its side.

दिगुत्तराभूदन्येयं पूर्वमेव महीधरः। 6/1.22.45

This reversal is said to have effected the change in the lodgings of the animate beings on the earth and as such the lodgings also shift sometimes to Vidhayan part of continents, sometimes to the Kaccha part and sometimes to the Sahya or Dardura parts of continents. It is shifted sometimes to glaciated part of continents and sometimes to Malaya part.

कदाचिदहमेकान्ते विन्ध्यकच्छकृतालयः।
कदाचित्सह्यनिलयः कदाचिद्दर्दुरालयः।। 6/1.22.39
कदाचिद् हिमवद्वासी कदाचिन्मलयाचलः।
कदाचित् प्राक्तनेनैव संनिवेशेन भूधरम्।। 6/1.22.40

What is Meru?

According to *Yogavāsiṣṭha* Meru is not a mountain, but the surface of the earth or say lithosphere is called Meru.

मेरुर्भूपीठः

At another place, Meru is used as an attributive of earth, which stands to mean earth qualified by meru or maru or sand.

मेरुर्धरा–5.41.31=

Thus Meru is symbolic of lithosphere and not of mountain.

Situation of Plakṣa Dvīpa

As per description of *Yogavāsiṣṭha* Plakṣa Dvīpa was encircled by the snowy plains of Himalayas.

ततो गोमेदकद्वीप लेखयैवं प्रमाणया।
इक्ष्वब्धि लेखयाप्येवं हिमवद्सानु शुद्धया। 3.25.22

Shape of Earth as looked from above

The earth appeared as a lotus in the heart of Brahmāṇḍa Puruṣa, the eight sides forming the petals of the flower, the clouds being its pistils and the pericarp containing its sweet flavour.

ब्रह्माण्डनर हृमद्मर्द्दिगष्टकदलवृहत्।
गिरिकेसर संबाधस्वामोदभरसुंदरम्।। 3.25.2

The earth like a lotus is situated on the surface of waters of oceans.

कदाचिदास्यदांमोधिकंपकंपितदिग्दलम्।

अधोनालगतानतदैत्यदानवकंटकम् ।। 3.25.6

Jambudvīpa

Jambudvīpa was the name of highly populated region according to *Yogavāsiṣṭha.*

लक्षयोजन विस्तीर्णानाकीर्णांचिरजो लबैः ।
नानाजनपदव्यूहस्थिरावश्याय सीकराम् ।। 3.25.13
स्थलेष्वामंडलांतस्थ जनजालालिमंडलाम् – 3.25.10

Kalpa Tree

The description of Kalpa tree as is available from *Yogavāsiṣṭha* gives one to understand (in spiritual sense) a tree of desire which branches out into various objects of our wish. Its flowers are all sanguine hopes and expectations which are hidden under the dark mist of futurity. The crown dwelling in its dark hollow, is the indwelling obscure Ātmā, which is hidden under the imperious gloom of our ignorant minds and false egotism. Its nest is in the highest divinity and it is immortal because it is a particle or Eternal spirit.

पुष्परेण्वभ्रवलितं रत्नस्तबकदन्तुरम् ।
उत्सेधनिर्जिताकाशं शृंगे शृंगमिवार्पितम् । 6/1.15.2

Its equivalent, in astronomical sense, is the sky with stars as its flowers, clouds as its leaves, flashes of lighting as its filaments circumvent beams of the radiant sun as the pollen of its flowers.

ताराद्विगुणपुष्पौघं मेघद्विगण पल्लवम् ।
रश्मिद्विगुण रेण्वभ्रं तडिद्द्विगुणमंजरीम् – 6/1.15.3

Purāṇas undergo interpolations

It has been made clear in the *Yogavāsiṣṭha* while recounting the past ages that *Purāṇas*, though agreeing in the main substance, are also full of interpolations, that they have been greatly multiplied in successive ages or *yugas.*

एकार्थानि समग्राणि बहुपाठानि मेऽनघ ।
पुराणानि प्रवर्तन्ते प्रसृतानि युगंप्रति ।। 6/1.22.20

Varied Readings and rituals of the Vedas

In the *Yogavāsiṣṭha*, it has been clarified that Vedas were subjected to various readings, as well as rituals from age to age, likewise the differences in the intellects of the scholars occurred from age to age. Vedas though remained intact so far as their internal structure was concerned but were subjected to various readings and rituals in various schools that emerged from time to time.

युगं प्रति धियां पुंसां न्यूनाधिकतया मुने।
क्रियांगपाठवैचित्र्ययुक्तान्वेदान्स्मराम्यहम्।। 6/1.22.19

Period of Rāma

Yogavāsiṣṭha also supplies the information regarding the time period of Rāma. In this connection following *śloka* may be referred to

अद्य राम कृते क्षीणे त्रेता सम्प्रति वर्तते – 6/1.27.18

From the above statement it is clear that during Rāma's time *Satyayuga* had elapsed and *Tretā* was in currency. According to the information of Mahābhārata Rāma was was born in the sandhi period of Dvāpara and Tretayuga[1]. Presently 28th Kaliyuga is in currency. As such the 28th Tretāyuga has passed.

However Puranic sources give a more specific information. Accordingly Rāma was born in the 24th Tretāyuga [2]. This period works out, given astronomical calculations, to be around 18 Million years. The calculations

---

1 संधौ तु समनुप्राप्ते त्रेताया द्वापरस्य च
रामो दाशरथिर्भूत्वा भविष्यामि जगत्पति।। 348.19 शा0 प0

2 त्रेतायुगे चतुर्विंशे रावणः तपसः क्षयात् ।
रामं दाश्रथिं प्राप्त सगणः क्षयमीयीवान् ।। वायुपुराण 70.88
चतुर्विंशे युगे वत्स त्रेतायां रघुवंशजः।
रामो नाम भविष्यामि चतुर्व्यूहः सनातनः।। ब्रह्माण्डपुराण 22.36.3
चतुर्विंशे युगे चापि विश्वामित्रपुरःसरः।
लोके राम इति ख्यातः तेजसा भास्करोपमः।। हरिवंश 22.104

are as under:

Years of 28th Kaliyuga elapsed	=5116
Years of 28th Dvāpara elapsed	=8,40,000
Years of 28th Tretā elapsed	=1296000
Years of 28th Satyayuga elapsed	=1728000
Years of 27th Mahāyuga elapsed	=4320000
Years of 26th Mahāyuga elapsed	=4320000
Years of 25th Mahāyuga elapsed	=4320000
Years of 24th Kaliyuga elapsed	=432000
Years of 24th Dvāpara elapsed	=8,40,000
Years of Sandhi of Dvāpara and Tretā	=108000

Total years elapsed	= 18209116

We have some more specific astronomical information about the birth of Rāma. Accordingly during the birth of Rāma vernal equinox used to take place in Punarvasu constellations. Presently vernal equinox takes place in Pūrva Bhādrapada constellations which has a precession of 117^0. It takes 117x 72= 8424 years for the precession of 117^0. As such nearest occurrence of vernal equinox in Punarvasu constellations comes about to be 6409 BC or Dvāpara 862693. The same cycle of vernal equinox to take place in Punarvasu constellations is repeated every 25920 years. From Dvāpara 862693 to the sandhi of 24th Tretā and Dvāpara, 702 precession cyles completes and the time period of Rāma in 24th Tretāyuga comes about 1818180 years ago. As such, period of Rāma as per Indian chronology 18 million years ago.[3] It is also mentioned in Purāṇas that by Rāma's time last phase of

---

[3] The scholars who try to work out the date of Rāma around 5000-6000 BC on the basis of planetarium soft ware forget that this combination of starts and planets is the latest one and the same combination is repeated every 25920 years.

Himalayan upliftment was also over. The above fact is corroborated by the internal evidence of Rāmāyaṇa and archeoloigcal findings. In Vālmīki Ramāyaṇa (Dr. Ravi Prakash Arya, 1998)[4], Sundara Kāṇḍa (4.27), it is mentioned that when Hanumāna first reached Rāvana's palace, he saw decked gateways surrounded by four tusked elephants resembling the masses of white clouds and wild beasts and birds. The verse goes like this:

वारणैश्च चतुर्दन्तैः श्वेताभ्रनिचयोपमैः।
भूषितैः रुचिरद्वारं मत्तैश्च मृगपक्षिभिः।।

At another place (Rāmāyaṇa, Sundara kāṇḍa, 27.12), Trijaṭā, a Rākṣasī, sees in her dream illustrious Rāma and Lakṣamaṇa mounted on huge elephant with four tusks and resembling a hill. The original verse reads as under:

राघवश्च पुनर्दृष्टश्चतुर्दन्त महागजम्।
आरूढः शैलसंकाशं चकास सहलक्ष्मणः।।

Mention of four tusked elephants by Vālmīki is a galring evidence of the fact that elephants with four tusks must have been present during the period of Rāmāyaṇa and Vālmīki. The Encarta Encyclopedia informs us about the presence of four-tusked elephants on earth between 38 million years ago to 15 million years ago. They are named as Mastodontoidea. Accordingly, Mastodontoidea evolved around 38 million years ago and became extinct about 15 million years ago when the shaggy and two tusked Mastodons increased in population.

The above proof lends a strong support to the authenticity of tradition of Purānas. Now one may easily understand that the astronomical time calculation system adopted by Vedic seers is only the key to the true chronology of India history. Whatever said or done in the name of modern calculations is quite misleading and proof of their misunderstanding of the Indian knowledge system.

---

[4] Dr. Ravi Prakash Arya (1998). Vālmiki Rāmāyaṇa edited with English Translation, (Four Vols.), Delhi

Four tusked elephant of Rāmāyaṇa

Similes in *Yogavāsiṣṭha*

We have heard a lot about the similes of Kālidāsa, but the similes of *Yogavāsiṣṭha* are no less remarkable even while elucidating the philosophical imports. To illustrate, one may quote here an example of impurity of heart being equated with the impurity of Gold.

कलंकयन्तः कलंकेन प्रोच्यते हेम नान्यथा।
भावासक्त्य समासक्त उक्तो जन्तुर्हि नान्यथा। 5.74.70

The gold becomes impure by its inward alloy, and not by its outward soil; so a man becomes unholy by the impurity of heart and foulness of his mind and not on account of dust or dirt on his body.

Authorship and date

The authorship of this great work is assigned to sage Valmīki, the famous author of Rāmāyaṇa. The *Viṣ-*

ṇudharmottara Purāṇa says that Vālmiki was born in the *Tretāyuga* as a form of Viṣṇu who composed the Rāmāyaṇa, and that people desirious of earning knowledge should worship Vālmiki[5]. He was contemporary to Rāma and the date of Rāma may also be the date of Vālmīki. This way Vālmīk's time may also be calculated minimum 900 thousand years ago and maximum 18 million years ago.

Yogavāsiṣṭha was composed by Ṛṣi Vālmīki after the composition of Rāmāyana was over. So the time period of first original composition Yogavāsiṣṭha by Vālmīki was also 900 thousands year (as per 28th Tretā) or 18 million years (as per 24th Tretā) ago. Present edition has reached us through thousand years long tradition.

Present Work

The present work titled as 'Yogavāsiṣṭha on Liberated Life' is the English translation of 11th Chapter of first part of Nirvāṇa Prakaraṇa of Yogavāsiṣṭha. This chapter is devoted to as to how to identify a liberated man. It sheds ample good light on the life and work style of a liberated person.

Having discussed the role of ajñāna in the bondage of human beings with the temporal world and ways of its release by means of proper insight and right reasoning, Rishi Vasiṣṭha cautions Rama that mere removal of ajñāna is not enough for the realization of Brahma until and unless repeated instructions are followed and translated into practice. When a person is able to attain Ātmajñāna, he is called Jivana Mukta, liberated while living. Main theme of *Yogavāsiṣṭha* is also realisation of Brahma. It is the most authoritative compendium showing deserving seeker a path to Ātmajñāna which ultimately leads a seeker to liberation, the sole motive of human life.

Since this chapter is very significant so far as the main theme of *Yogavāsiṣṭha* is concerned, Valmiki Research Unit of Shri Guru Valmik Sabha, Southhall, Middlesex, England, UB2

---

[5] Mythology of Vishnu and His Incarnations by Manohar Laxman Varadpande (2009), p. 166

5AA wants to publish the above chapter with an authentic English, Hindi and Punjabi translations for the public at large and Shri Guru Valmik Mandirs in particular. Therefore, Sh. P. L. Soba of Valmiki Research Unit of Shri Guru Valmik Sabha, Southhall, Middlesex, England, UB2 5AA approached the author of present lines to produce the above chapter with an authentic translations into English, Hindi and Punjabi languages, so that this work on Vedanta philosophy may become accessible both to the readers and seekers alike who are not well versed with Sanskrit Language. He gave some suggestions regarding the production of this work, so that even a layman can understand the sublime philosophy of *Yogavāsiṣṭha.* Accordingly, the present work quotes original Sanskrit Śloka in Devanāgarī alongwoth its transliteration in Roman followed by meaning of Sanskrit words in English and finally the translation in English. The technical terms of *Yogavāsiṣṭha* have no corresponding terms in other languages, so they have been written as it is with their definitions, so that the readers may not find any difficulty to understand their imports. A glossry of technical terms has also been given at the end of this book, so that the readers may refer to it to clear their doubts.

Here it may not be out of context to point out that the available editions of *Yogavāsiṣṭha* although produced by their authors with utmost possible care and precise translations in Hindi or English, have largely failed to comprehend the analogical depiction and actual and factual intended sense of its original author, Valmiki. The author of present lines himself edited way back in 1998 English translation of Vihari Lal Mitra rendered by him in 1881. Although it has the credit of being the first ever complete English translation of *Yogavāsiṣṭha,* but it can never claim the credit of being perfect and precise English translation. At many places it has become so mysterious and misleading that the readers are unable to understand the actual intended sense of the original author. As such, an objective and updated translation is the dire need of the hour. Keeping in view of the same need, an objective approach has been followed in the present edition to reflect the actual intention of the original author, rather than reading pre-conceived notions into its verses and projecting his own ideas in the name of meanings of various verses. It has been tried at the level best that the original meaning of the verses of *Yogavāsiṣṭha* is not superimposed by speculated meaning and its true sense is plucked out to the gaze of all. Hope this translation will prove first ever attempt to project the true spirit of *Yogavāsiṣṭha* in English language. It is also hoped that readers and seekers will be benefited alike with this great philosophical work produced first ever in the history of humankind by the great sage of the land, Valmīki.

Dr. Ravi Prakash Arya
114, Akash, DRDO Complex,
Lucknow Road, Timarpur, Delhi-110054
Ph. 09313033917;09650183260; 011-65188114; 011-23814323
Email : vedicscience@rediffmail.com
vedicscience@hotmail.com
Website : www.vedascience.com

MAṄGLĀCARAṆ
(DIVINE ADORATION)

यतः सर्वाणि भूतानि प्रतिभान्ति स्थितानि च।
यत्रैवोपशमं यान्ति तस्मै सत्यात्मने नमः।।१।।

yataḥ sarväṇi bhūtäni pratibhänti sthitäni ca
yatraivopaśamaṁ yänti tasmai satyätmane namaḥ.

यतः *yataḥ=from whom*
सर्वाणि भूतानि *sarväṇi bhūtäni=all living and non-living beings*
प्रतिभान्ति *pratibhänti= spring forth*
स्थितानि च *sthitäni ca= and stay*
यत्रैव उपशमं यान्ति *yatraiva upaśamaṁ yānti= submerge in the end*
तस्मै सत्यात्मने नमः *tasmai satyätmane namaḥ=Salutations to ever-existent Parmātmā*

Salutations to the Ever existent Parmātmā from whom spring forth living and non-living beings, in whom they stay and submerge in the end.

ज्ञाताज्ञानं तथा ज्ञेयं द्रष्टा दर्शनदृश्यभूः।
कर्त्ता हेतुः क्रिया यस्मात्तस्मै ज्ञप्त्यात्मने नमः।।२।।

jñätä jñänaṁ tathä jñeyaṁ draṣṭä darśana dṛśyabhūḥ
karttä hetuḥ kriyä yasmät tasmai jñaptyätmane namaḥ.

ज्ञाता *jñätä= knower*
ज्ञानम् *jñänaṁ= knowledge*
तथा ज्ञेयम् *tathä jñeyaṁ= and knowable*

द्रष्टा *drașțä= seer*

दर्शन *darśana=sight*

दृश्यभूः *dṛśyabhūḥ=and observer space/visible universe*

कर्त्ता *karttä= doer*

हेतुः *hetuḥ= cause*

क्रिया *kriyä=action*

यस्मात् *yasmät = from whom spring forth*

तस्मै ज्ञप्त्यात्मने नमः *tasmai jñaptyätmane namaḥ=salutations to Parmātmā of the nature of pure intelligence (electric/bio electric current)*

Salutations to Parmātmā of the nature of pure intelligence (electric/bio-electric current) from whom spring forth knower, knowledge and knowable; seer, sight and visible universe; doer, cause and action.

स्फुरन्ति सीकरा यस्मादानन्दस्याम्बरे
सर्वेषां जीवनं तस्मै ब्रह्मात्मने नमः ।।३।।

sphuranti sīkarä yasmäd änandasyämbare
sarveṣäṁ jīvanaṁ tasmai brahmätmane namaḥ.

स्फुरन्ति *sphuranti= spring forth*

सीकरा *sīkarä= sprays*

यस्माद *yasmäd= from whom*

आनन्दस्य *änandasya= of bliss*

अम्बरे *ambare= in heaven*

सर्वेषां जीवनम् *sarveṣäṁ jīvanam= life of all*

तस्मै ब्रह्मात्मने नमः *tasmai brahmätmane namaḥ=Salutations to Parmātmā*

Salutations to Parmātmā from whom spring forth sprays of bliss in heaven and who is the life of all.

NIRVĀṆA PRAKARAṆA
Uttarārdha (Part 2)
Chapter 11

(DISCOURSE ON LIBERATED LIFE)

Having discussed the role of ajñāna in the bondage of human beings with the temporal world and ways of its release by means of proper insight and right reasoning, Rishi Vasiṣṭha cautions Rama that mere removal of ajñāna is not enough for the liberation until and unless repeated instructions followed and translated into practice.

वसिष्ठ उवाच
Vasiṣṭha Said

पुनः पुनरिदं राम प्रबोधार्थं मयोच्यते।
अभ्यासेन विना साधो नाभ्युदेत्यात्मभावना।।१।।

punaḥ punaridam rāma prabodhārthaṁ mayocyate
abhyāsena vinā sādho nābhyudety-ātma-bhāvanā.

पुनः पुनरिदम punaḥ punaridam = repeatedly
राम Rāma = O Rama
प्रबोधार्थं prabodhārthaṁ = for understanding
मयोच्यते mayocyate = I tell you
अभ्यासेन विना abhyāsena vine = without repeated practice

साधो sādho= accomplished
न अभ्युदेति आत्मभावना nābhyudety-ātma-bhāvanā= Ātma jñāna (realization of actual nature of ātmā) does not arise

Vasiṣṭha Said: I tell you Repeatedly O accomplished Rama! for your understanding. *Ātma jñāna* does not arise without repeated practice.

अज्ञानमेतद् बलवदविद्येतरनामकम।
जन्मान्तरसहस्रोत्थं घनं स्थितिमुपागतम्।।२।।

ajñānam etad balavad avidyetara nāmakam
janmāntara sahasraortharṁ ghanaṁ sthitimupāgatam.

अज्ञानम् एतद ajñānam etad= it is the ajñāna (absence of proper and precise information about Ātmā and Paramātmā). Note Ātmā remains confined to one single living body, but Paramātmā pervades whole living and non-living world.
बलवद् balavad= powerful
अविद्या इतरनामकम avidyā itara nāmakam= known as avidyā
जन्मान्तर–सहस्रोत्थ janmāntara sahasraorthaṁ= owes its origin to numerous past lives
घनं स्थितिम् उपागतम् ghanaṁ sthitim upāgatam= assumed such a solid state

It is the *ajñāna*, known as *avidyā*, which is a powerful barrier to Ātma jñāna and Brahma Jñāna (realization of Ātmā and Paramātmā). This *ajñāna* has assumed a compact state owing its origin to numerous past lives.

स बाह्याभ्यन्तरं सर्वैरिन्द्रियैरनुभूयते।
भावाभावेषु देहस्य तेनातिघनतां गतम्।।३।।

sa bāhyābhyantaraṁ sarvairindriyair anubhūyate.
bhāvābhāveṣu dehasya tenatighanatāṁ gatam.

स sa= this ajñāna

***बाह्य आभ्यन्तरम्** bāhyābhyantaram = external body senses (five senses) and internal body sense (mind)*
***सर्वैर् इन्द्रियैर् अनुभूयते** sarvairindriyair anubhūyate = accumulated through sense organs*
***भाव–अभावेषु देहस्य** bhāvābhāveṣu dehasya = body's state of consciousness and unconsciousness.*
***तेन** tena = this is also one of the reason*
***अतिघनतां गतम्** tighanatāṁ gatam = has become grossly compacted one*

This *ajñāna* has become grossly compacted one, as it is always accumulated through external (five senses) and internal (mind) body senses, both in the states of consciousness and unconsciousness.

आत्मज्ञानं तु सर्वेषामिन्द्रियाणामगोचरम् ।
सत्तां केवलमायाति मनःषष्ठेन्द्रियक्षये ।।४।।

ātmajñānaṁ tu sarveṣām indriyāṇām-agocaram.
sattāṁ kevalam āyāti manaḥ ṣaṣṭhendriya-kṣaye.

***आत्मज्ञानम्** ātmajñānam = Ātma jñāna (realization of self)*
***सर्वेषाम् इन्द्रियाणाम् अगोचरम्** sarveṣām indriyāṇām-agocaram = a subject beyond the reach of all senses*
***सत्तां केवलम् आयाति** sattāṁ kevalam āyāti = It takes place only*
***मनः षष्ठेन्द्रिय–क्षये** manaḥ = manas including five sense organs are controlled.*

Ātma jñāna is a subject far beyond the reach of sense organs. It *(Ātmajñāna)* is attained only when five external sense organs including *manas* are restrained.

प्रोल्लंघयेन्द्रियजां वृत्तिं यत्स्थितं तत्कथं किल ।
याति प्रत्यक्षतां जन्तोः प्रत्यक्षातीतवृत्तिमत् ।।।५।।

prollaṅghayendriyajāṁ vṛttiṁ yatsthitaṁ tatkathaṁ kila.

yāti pratyakṣatāṁ jamtoḥ pratyakṣātīta vṛttimat.

प्रोल्लंघय इन्द्रियजां वृत्तिं *prollaṅghayendriyajāṁ vṛttiṁ= beyond the jurisdiction of sensory perception.*
यत्स्थितम् *yatsthitaṁ= which exists*
तत्कथं किल *tatkathaṁ kila= How than is it possible?*
याति प्रत्यक्षताम् *yāti pratyakṣatāṁ= revealed*
जन्तोः *jamtoḥ= seeker*
प्रत्यक्षातीत–वृत्तिमत् *pratyakṣātīta vṛttimat= power to perceive beyond senses*

How is it possible to attain *Ātma jñāna* which is beyond the jurisdiction of sensory perception. It is revealed only to those seekers who have the power to perceive beyond the senses.

त्वमविद्यालतामेतां प्ररूढां हृदयद्रुमे।
ज्ञानाभ्यास विलासासिपातैच्छिन्द्ध स्वसिद्धये।।६।।

tvamavidyālatām etāṁ prarūḍhāṁ hṛdayadrume.
jñānābhyāsavilāsāsipātaicchindha svasiddhaye.

त्वम् *tvam=you*
अविद्यालताम् एताम् *avidyālatām etāṁ=* this creeper of *ajñāna*
प्ररूढाम् *prarūḍhāṁ=* grown up
हृदयद्रुमे *hṛdayadrume=* in the tree of heart
ज्ञानाभ्यास विलास–असि–पातैः *jñānābhyāsavilāsāsipātaiḥ=* with the sharp sword of jñāna (proper and precise knowledge of *Ātmā* and *Parmātmā*) practiced by you
छिन्द्ध स्वसिद्धये *chindha svasiddhaye=* cut off for seeking self

You must cut off this creeper of *ajñāna* which has grown up on the tree of your heart with the sharp sword of *jñāna* practiced by you for the sake of Ātma jñāna.

यथा विहरति ज्ञातज्ञेयो जनकभूपतिः ।
आत्मज्ञानाभ्यासपरस्तथा विहर राघव ।।७।।

yathā viharati jñātajñeyo Janaka-bhūpatiḥ
ātmajñānābhyāsaparastathā vihara Rāghava.

यथा *yathā = in the manner*
विहरति *viharati = conducts*
ज्ञातज्ञेयः *jñātajñeyaḥ = with you full knowledge of all that is knowable to man*
जनकभूपतिः *Janaka-bhūpatiḥ = king Janaka*
आत्मज्ञान–आभ्यासपरः *ātmajñānābhyāsaparaḥ = seeking practice of Ātma jñāna*
तथा *tathā = in the same manner*
विहर *vihara = conduct yourself*
राघव *Rāghava = O'Raghava!*

O Raghava! conduct the practice of *Ātma jñāna* with your full knowledge of all that is knowable to man, as was done by king Janaka.

निश्चयोऽयमभूत्तस्य कार्याकार्ये विहारिणः ।
जाग्रतस्तिष्ठतो वाऽपि तज्ज्ञानं तेन सत्यता ।।८।।

niścayo'yam-abhūttasya kāryākārye vihāriṇaḥ
jāgratastiṣṭhato vā'pi tajjñānaṁ tena satyatā.

निश्चयः अयम् अभूत् तस्य *niścayo'yam abhūttasya = He was confirmed about this fact*
कार्ये अकार्ये विहारिणः *kārya-akārye vihāriṇaḥ = to conduct worldly and spiritual affairs*
जाग्रतः *jāgratas = while in waking state*
तिष्ठतः *tiṣṭhataḥ = while in samādhi (focused state of mind)*
वा अपि *vā'pi =*

तत् ज्ञानं =*tajjñānaṁ* = *Self realisarion*
तेन सत्यता *tajjñānaṁ tena satyatā* = *key to know ultimate reality*

King Janak, who was able to conduct worldly affairs while in waking state and spiritual afairs while in Samādhi, was also confirmed about this fact (that *Ātma jñāna* is the result of continuous practice) and that same (*Ātma jñāna*) is the only key to *Brahma Jñāna* (knowledge of the Parmātmā).

निश्चयेन हरिर्येन विविधाचारकारिणा।
योनिष्ववतरत्युर्व्यां तत्तज्ज्ञत्वमुदाहृतम्।।९।।

niścayena hariryena vividhācārakāriṇā
yoniṣv-avataraty-urvyāṁ tat-tajjña-tvam udāhṛtam.

निश्चयेन *niścayena*= confirmation
हरिर् *harir*=Hari
येन *yena* = by
विविधाचार–कारिणा *vividhācārakāriṇā*= to perform various worldly affairs
योनिषु *yoniṣu*= many past lives
अवतरति *avatarati*= takes birth
उर्व्याम् *urvyām* = on the earth
तत् तज्ज्ञत्वम् उदाहृतम् *tat-tajjñatvam udāhṛtam*= This is also a proof of the above fact

It is by reliance on the confirmation of the above fact that Ātmajñāna is the result of continuous practice observed during many past lives, Hari (Vishnu) was led to take many births and perform worldly affairs. This could be deemed as a proof.

निश्चयोयस्त्रिनेत्रस्य कान्तया सह तिष्ठतः।
ब्राह्मणो वाऽप्यरागस्य स ते भवतु राघव।।१०।।

niścayo-yas-trinetrasya kāntayā saha tiṣṭhataḥ
brāhmaṇo vāpyarāgasya sa te bhavatu rāghava.

निश्चयः *niścayaḥ* = confirmation
यः *yaḥ* = same
त्रिनेत्रस्य *trinetrasya* = Śiva
कान्तया सह तिष्ठतः *kāntayā saha tiṣṭhataḥ* = accompanied by his wife
ब्राह्मणः वा अपि *brāhmaṇaḥ vā api* = Brahmā also
अरागस्य *arāgasya* = devoid of all kinds of attachments
स ते भवतु राघव *sa te bhavatu rāghava* = You may also have the same experience O Rama!

Śiva accompanied by his wife Parvati is also confirmed about it. Similar is the opinion of Brahmā who is devoid of all kinds of attachments. You may also have the same experience O Rama! the descendant of Raghu.

यो निश्चयः सुरगुरोर्वाक्पतेर्भार्गवस्य च।
दिवाकरस्य शशिनः पवनस्याऽनलस्य च।। ११।।

yo niścayaḥ surgurorvākpaterbhārgavasya ca
divākarasya śaśinaḥ pavansyānalasya ca.

यो निश्चयः *yo niścayaḥ* = similar conclusion
सुरगुरोः *surguroḥ* = of Bṛhaspati, Guru of Devas (people dwelling in the eastern horizon of earth)
वाक्पतेः *vākpater* = of Vākpati
भार्गवस्य च *bhārgavasya ca* = of son of Bhṛgu
दिवाकरस्य *divākarasya* =of Divākara
शशिनः *śaśinaḥ* = of ŚaśI
पवनस्य *pavansyā* = of Pavana
अनलस्य च *analasya ca* = of Anala

Bṛhaspati, Guru of Devas (people dwelling in the eastern

horizon of earth), Vākpati, son of Bhṛgu, Divākara, ŚaśI, Pavana and Anala had similar conclusions.

नारदस्य पुलस्त्यस्य मम चांऽगिरसस्तथा।।
प्रचेतसो भृगोश्चैव क्रतोरत्रेः शुकस्य च।। १२।।

nāradasya pulastyasya mama cāṅgirasastathā
pracetaso bhṛgoścaiva kratoratreḥ śukrasya ca.

नारदस्य *Nāradasya = of Narada*
पुलस्त्यस्य *Pulastyasya = of Pulastya*
मम च *mama cā = including me*
अंगिरसस्तथा *Aṅgirasastathā = as well as that of Aṅgiras*
प्रचेतसो *Pracetaso = of Pracetas*
भृगोश्चैव *Bhṛgoścaiva = and that of Bhṛgu*
क्रतोः *Kratoḥ = of Kratu*
अत्रेः *Atreḥ = of Atri*
शुकस्य च *Śukrasya ca = and that of Śukra*

The opinion of Narada, Pulstya including me, as well as that of Aṅgiras, Pracetā, Bhṛgu, Kratu, Atri and that of Śukrācārya is no different from others.

अन्येषामेव विप्रेन्द्रराजर्षीणां च राघव।
यो निश्चयो विमुक्तानां जीवतां ते भवत्वसौ।। १३।।

anyeṣāmeva viprendrarājarṣīṇāṁ ca rāghav.
yo niścayo vimuktānāṁ jīvatāṁ te bhavatvasau.

अन्येषाम् एव *anyeṣāmeva = others'*
विप्रेन्द–राजर्षीणां च *viprendra-rājarṣīṇāṁ ca = of eminent scholars and sage kings*
राघव *Rāghav = O Rāma!*
यः निश्चयः *yaḥ niścayaḥ = confirm*

विमुक्तानां जीवताम् vimuktānāṁ jīvatāṁ= of those who attained liberation in their life time
ते भवतु असौ te bhavatvasau = The same may be had by you

This was also confirmed by all other eminent scholars, Rājarṣis (sage-kings) and by all those who attained liberation in their life time. The same may be had by you O' Rāma!

श्रीराम उवाच
Śri Rāma Said

येनैते भगवन् धीरा निश्चयेन महाधियः।
विशोकाः संस्थितास्तन्मे ब्रह्मन्प्रब्रूहि तत्त्वतः।।१४।।

yenaite bhagvan dhīrā niścayena mahādhiyaḥ
viśokāḥ sansthitāstanme Brahman prabrūhi tattvataḥ.

येन yena = which
एते ete = those
भगवन् bhagvan = venerable
धीरा dhīrā =sages
निश्चयेन niścayena= with confirmation
महाधियः mahādhiyaḥ = high profile scholars
विशोकाः संस्थिताः viśokāḥ sansthitāḥ = become relieved of berievement and sorrow
तन् tan = that
मे me = me
ब्रह्मन् Brahman = sage
प्रब्रूहि तत्त्वतः prabrūhi tattvataḥ = tell truly

Śri Rāma said: Tell me truly with confirmation, O venerable sage, about the conclusion arrived at by these high profile scholars and sages, based upon which they have become relieved of berievement and sorrow.

वसिष्ठ उवाच
Vasiṣṭha Said

राजपुत्र महाबाहो विदिताखिलवेद्य हे।
स्फुटं शृणु यथा पृष्टमयमेषां हि निश्चयः।।१५।।

rājputra mahābāgo viditākhilavedya he
sphuṭaṁ śṛṇu yathā pṛṣṭamayameṣāṁ hi niścayaḥ

राजपुत्र महाबाहो *rājputra mahābāgo = Long armed worthy prince*
विदिताखिलवेद्य हे! *viditākhilavedya he= you have the knowledge of all that is knowable*
स्फुटं शृणु *sphuṭaṁ śṛṇu = Listen me clearly*
यथा पृष्टम् *yathā pṛṣṭam = as asked by you*
अयम् एषां हि निश्चयः *ayameṣāṁ hi niścayaḥ= about the conclusion arrived at by them*

Vasiṣṭha Said: O long armed worthy prince! you have the knowledge of all that is knowable. Listen me clearly, as asked by you, about the conclusion arrived at by all of them.

यदिदं किंचिदाभोगि जगज्जालं प्रदृश्यते।
तत्सर्वममलं ब्रह्म भवत्येतद्व्यवस्थितम्।।१६।।

yadidaṁ kiñcidābhogi jagajjālaṁ pradṛśyate
tatsarvamamalaṁ brahma bhavatyetad vyavasthitam.

यदिदम् *yad idaṁ= All this*
किंचिद् आभोगि जगज्जालम् *kiñcid ābhogi jagajjālaṁ= extensive network of worlds*
प्रदृश्यते *pradṛśyate=visible*
तत्सर्वम् अमलं ब्रह्म *tatsarvam amalaṁ brahma= All that is pervaded by stainless Brahma*

भवति एतद् व्यवस्थितम् *bhavati etad vyavasthitam= It is an established view*

All this visible extensive network of worlds is pervaded by stainless Brahma. It is an established view.

ब्रह्म चिद्ब्रह्म भुवनं ब्रह्म भूतपरम्पराः।
ब्रह्माऽहं ब्रह्म मच्छत्रुर्ब्रह्म सन्मित्रबान्धवाः।
ब्रह्म कालत्रयं तच्च ब्रह्मण्येव व्यवस्थितम्।। १७।।

brahm cidbrahm bhuvanaṁ brahma bhūtaparamparāḥ
brahmā'haṁ brahm macchatrurbrahma sanmitra bāndhavāḥ.
brahma kālatrayaṁ tacca brahmaṇyeva vyavasthitam

ब्रह्म चिद् brahma cid= embodied. Cid Brahma refers here embodied Brahma that pervades all animate and inanimate bodies. Embodied Brahma or cetanā is identifiable as intelligence which is electric charge in inanimate world and bio-electric charge in animate world. Inanimate bodies are devoid of Ātmā, but animate bodies have Ātmā. So inanimate bodies can have only intelligence, but animate bodies have both intelligence as well as consciousness)

ब्रह्म भुवनम् brahma bhuvanaṁ brahma = Brahma pervades entire universe

ब्रह्म भूतपरम्पराः brahma bhūta-paramparāḥ= Brahma pervades animate beings and inanimate objects

ब्रह्म अहं brahma ahaṁ = Brahma pervades me

ब्रह्म मत् शत्रुर् brahma mat śatrur = Brahma pervades my foes

ब्रह्म सन्मित्रबान्धवाः Brahma sanmitra bāndhavāḥ = Brahma pervades my friends and relativs

ब्रह्म कालत्रयम् *brahma kālatrayaṁ= Brahma pervades all three forms of time - past, present and future*

तत् च ब्रह्मणि एव व्यवस्थितम् tacca brahmaṇyeva vyavasthitam= that time is placed in Brahma

Brahma is pure. Brahma pervades entire universe, He

pervades all animate and inanimate bodies. He pervades me, my relatives, foes and friends. He pervades all the three forms of time and time is placed in Brahma.

तरंगमालयाऽम्भोधिर्यथाऽऽत्मनिविवर्धते।
तथा पदार्थलक्ष्म्येत्थमिदं ब्रह्म विवर्धते। ।१८।।

taranmālayā'mbhodhiryathātmanivivardhate.
tathā padarthalakṣmyetthamidaṁ brahma vivardhate

तरंग—मालया *taraṅ-mālayā= waves*
अम्भोधि यथा *ambhodhir yathā= as contained in ocean*
आत्मनि *ātmani= contained in Ātmā*
विवर्धते *vivardhate =finds its expansion*
तथा *tathā= similarly*
पदार्थलक्ष्म्या इत्थम् *padartha-lakṣmyā ittham= thus through material world*
इदं ब्रह्म विवर्धते *idaṁ brahma vivardhate= this Brahma expands*

Just as an ocean finds its expansion in the waves contained in it. Similarly, Brahma finds His expansion in the material world/universe contained in it.

गृह्यते ब्रह्मणा ब्रह्म भुज्यते ब्रह्म ब्रह्मणा।
ब्रह्म ब्रह्मणि बृंहाभिर्ब्रह्मशक्त्येव बृंहति।। १६।।

gṛhyate brahmaṇā brahma bhujyate brahma brahmaṇā.
brahma brahmaṇi bṛṅhābhir brahmaśaktyeva bṛṅhati

गृह्यते ब्रह्मणा ब्रह्म *gṛhyate brahmaṇā brahma= Brahma conceives universe during creation*
भुज्यते ब्रह्म ब्रह्मणा *bhujyate brahma brahmaṇā= Brahma consumes universe during dissolution*
ब्रह्म ब्रह्मणि *brahma brahmaṇi= universe resides in Brahma*

बृंहाभिर् ब्रह्मशक्त्या इव *bṛṅhābhir brahmaśaktyā iva= expanding power of Brahma*
बृंहति *bṛṅhati= expands*

Brahma conceives universe during creation phase and and consumes universe during dissolution phase. Universe resides in Brahma upon its creation and expands by expanding power of Brahma.

ब्रह्म मच्छत्रुरूपं मे ब्रह्मणोऽप्रियकृद्यदि।
तद्ब्रह्मणि ब्रह्मनिष्ठं किमन्यत् कस्यचित्कृतम्।। २०।।

brahma macchatru rūpaṁ me brahmaṇo'priyakṛdyadi.
tad brahmaṇi brahmaniṣṭhaṁ kimanyat kasyacitkṛtam

ब्रह्म मत् शत्रुरूपम् *brahma mat śatru rūpaṁ= Brahma has pervaded my enemy*
मे ब्रह्मणः *me brahmaṇaḥ = Brahma has pervaded me*
अप्रियकृद् यदि *apriyakṛd yadi= if some harm is done by my enemy to me*
तद् *tad= that*
ब्रह्मणि ब्रह्मनिष्ठं *brahmaṇi brahmaniṣṭhaṁ= will be done by Brahma unto Brahma*
किमन्यत् कस्यचित् कृतम् *kimanyat kasyacit kṛtam= who else does whose harm? i.e. nobody does harm to anybody*

Brahma has pervaded me and my enemy. If some harm is done by my enemy to me, that will be considered a harm done by Brahma unto Brahma. Nobody does harm to any body.

रागादीनामवस्थानं कल्पितानां खवृक्षवत्।
असंकल्पेन नष्टानां कः प्रसंगोऽत्र वर्धते।।२१।।

rāgādīnāmavasthānaṁ kalpitānāṁ khavṛkṣavat.
asaṅkalpena naṣṭānāṁ kaḥ prasaṅgo'tra vardhate

रागादीनाम् अवस्थानं *rāgādīnāmavasthānaṁ= attribution of passions like rāga (attachment),* dveṣa *(enmity) etc.*
कल्पितानाम् *kalpitānām= imaginary*
खवृक्षवत् *khavṛkṣavat= plant in a sky*
असंकल्पेन नष्टानाम् *asaṅkalpena naṣṭānām= non-existent for want of desire*
कः प्रसंगः अत्र वर्धते *kaḥ prasaṅgaḥ atra vardhate= question of their development is irrelevant*

The attribution of imaginary passions like rāga (attachment/friendship), *dveṣa* (enmity) etc. to Brahma is like planting of a tree in sky. These passions are non-existent in Brahma for want of any desire in Him for them. So the question of their development in Brahma is irrelevant.

ब्रह्मण्येव हि सर्वस्मिंश्चरणस्पन्दनादिकम्।
स्फुरति ब्रह्म सकलं सुखितादुःखिते कुतः।। २२।।

brāhmaṇyeva hi sarvasminṣcaraṇaspandanādikam.
sphurati brahma sakalaṁ sukhitāduḥkhite kutaḥ

ब्रह्माणि एव हि *brāhmaṇi eva hi =in Brahma only*
सर्वस्मिन् चरणस्पन्दनादिकम् *sarvasminṣcaraṇaspandanādikam= everything moves*
स्फुरति *sphurati = pervades*
ब्रह्म *brahma = Brahma*
सकलम् *sakalaṁ =everything*
सुखितादुःखिते कुतः *sukhitāduḥkhite kutaḥ=so the question of pleasure and pain doesn't arise*

Everthig moves in Brahma only and Brahma pervades everything in a uniform manner, so the question of pleasure and pain doesn't arise.

ब्रह्म ब्रह्मणि संतृप्तं ब्रह्म ब्रह्मणि संस्थितम्।
स्फुरति ब्रह्मणि ब्रह्म नाहमस्मीतरात्मकः।। २३।।

brahma brhmaṇi santṛptaṁ brahma brahmaṇi sansthitam
sphurati brahmaṇi brahma nā'hamasmītarātmakaḥ

ब्रह्म ब्रह्मणि संतृप्तम् *brahma brhmaṇi santṛptam= Brahma contends in itself*
ब्रह्म ब्रह्मणि संस्थितम् *brahma brahmaṇi sansthitam= Brahma resides in itself*
स्फुरति ब्रह्मणि ब्रह्म *sphurati brahmaṇi brahma= Brahma pervades Brahma*
न अहम् अस्मि इतरात्मकः *na aham asmi itarātmakaḥ= Me too is not pervaded by other element than Brahma*

Brahma contends in Himself and resides in Himself. No other but Brahma pervades Himself. Me too is not pervaded by other element than Brahma.

घटो ब्रह्म पटो ब्रह्म ब्रह्माहमिदमाततम्।
अतो रागविरागाणां मृषेव कलनेह का।। २४।।

ghaṭo brahma paṭo brahma brahmā'gamidamātatam
ato rāgavirāgāṇāṁ mṛṣeva kalaneha kā

घटः ब्रह्म *ghaṭo brahma= pot is pervaded by Brahma*
पटः ब्रह्म *paṭo brahma=cloth is pervaded by Brahma*
ब्रह्म अहम् इदम् आततम् *brahma aham idam ātatam =me too is pervaded by Brahma*
अतो *ato = hence*
रागविरागाणाम् *rāga-virāgāṇāṁ= notions of attachment and aversion*
मृषा इव कलना इह का *mṛṣā iva kalanā iha kā= it is vain to imagin here*

This pot, that cloth and me too is pervaded by Brahma. Hence, it is vain to imagin here of notions like attachment and aversion.

मरण ब्रह्मणि स्वैरं देहब्रह्मणि संगते।
दुःखितानाम कैव स्याद्रज्जुसर्पभ्रमोपमा।। २५।।

maraṇa brahmaṇi svairaṁ dehabrahmaṇi saṅgate.
duḥkhitānām kaiva syād rajju-sarpa-bhramopamā

मरण ब्रह्मणि *maraṇa brahmaṇi= mortality*
स्वैरम् *vairaṁ = by nature*
देहब्रह्मणि संगते *dehabrahmaṇI saṅgate= when associated with physical body*
दुःखितानाम *duḥkhitānām=pain*
कैव स्याद् *kaiva syād = how can take place*
रज्जुसर्पभ्रमोपमा *rajjusarpabhramopamā= like fear of serpant in rope caused by a false perception.*

When mortality is associated with physical body by nature, and Ātmā never never dies. How can pain take place? The imagination of pain in physical body is illusory like that of a fear of serpant in rope caused by false perception.

Note: pain is experienced because of proximity of prakṛti (body) and body is mortal, so pain is non existent in body like a false fear of serpant in a rope.

सम्भोगादौ सुखं ब्रह्मण्यास्थिते देहब्रह्मणि।
सम्पन्नमेतन्म इति मुधा स्यात्कलना कुतः।। २६।।

sambhogādau sukhaṁ brahmaṇyāsthite deha brahmaṇi
sampannam etan-me iti mudhā syāt kalanā kutaḥ

सम्भोगादौ *sambhogādau= during sex*
सुखम् *sukhaṁ= orgasm*
ब्रह्मणि आस्थिते देहब्रह्मणि *brahmaṇyāsthite deha brahmaṇi= Because of presence of Brahma in embodied Ātmā. Ātmā when occupies a body called embodied Ātmā,*
सम्पन्नम् एतत् मे *sampannam etat me= it (orgasm) happened in me*
इति मुधा स्यात् कलना कुतः *iti mudhā syāt kalanā kutaḥ= it is a vain imagination*

Orgasm during sex is caused, because of presence of Brahma in embodied *Ātmā*. It (orgasm) happened in me (my body), is a vain imagination.

Note: pleasure is caused because of presence of Ātmā and not of body.

वीच्यम्भसोः स्पन्दवतोर्न त्वन्यदम्बुनो यथा।
त्वत्तामत्ते तथा न स्तो ब्रह्मणि स्पन्दरूपिणि।। २७।।

vicyambhasoḥ spandavatorna tvanyadambuno yathā.
tvattāmatte tathā na sto brahmaṇi spandarupiṇi

वीचि–अम्भसोः *vici ambhasoḥ= wave and water*
स्पन्दवतोः *spandavatoḥ= being under vibrations*
न तु अन्यद् अम्बुनः यथा *na tvanyadambuno yathā= as wave is not different from water*
त्वत्ता–मत्ते तथा न स्तः *tvattā-matte tathā na staḥ= so distinction between yourself and myself cannot persist*
ब्रह्मणि स्पन्दरूपिणि *brahmaṇi spandarupiṇi= when they exist pulsating in Brahma*

As water and wave, when both being under vibrations, one (the wave) is not distinguishable from another (water), so distinction between yourself and myself (individual Ātmā-s) cannot persist when they exist together pulsating in Paramātmā.

यथाऽऽवर्तमृते तोये न किंचिन्म्रियते क्वचित्।
मृतिब्रह्मत्वमायाते देहब्रह्मणि वै तथा।। २८।।

yathā'varta-mṛte toye na kincin-mriyate kvacit
mṛtibrahmatvam āyāte dehabrahmaṇī vai tathā

यथा आवर्तमृते तोये *yathā āvarta-mṛte toye= when whirlpool subsides in waters*
न किंचित् म्रियते क्वचित् *na kincit-mriyate kvacit= nothing gets destroyed anywhere*
मृति *mṛti = upon death*
ब्रह्मत्वम् आयाते *brahmatvam āyāte= merges with Brahma*
देहब्रह्मणि वै तथा *dehabrahmaṇī vai tathā= so embodied Ātmā*

As nothing gets destroyed anywhere in waters when whirlpool subsides. So, embodied Ātmā merges with Brahma upon death of body and never gets destroyed.

यथा चलाचले तोये त्वत्तामत्ते न तिष्ठतः।
तथा जडाजडे रूपे न स्थिते परमात्मनि।। २६।।

yathā calācale toye tvattāmatte na tiṣṭhataḥ
tathā jaḍājaḍe rūpe na sthite paramātmani

यथा *yathā= just as*
चलाचले तोये *cala- acale toye = moving and still waters*
त्वत्ता–मत्ते न तिष्ठतः *tvattā-matte na tiṣṭhataḥ= distinction of this or that*
तथा *tathā = similarly*
जडाजडे रूपे *tathā jaḍa-ajaḍe rūpe= gross matter and sentient beings*
न *na = no longer*

स्थिते परमात्मनि *na sthite paramātmani= exist in Paramātmā (Brahma)*

Just as no distinction is possible in moving and unmoving waters. Similarly, distinction of Jaḍa (gross matter) and ajaḍa (sentient beings) no longer persists while they exist in Paramātmā.

कटकत्वं यथा हेम्नो यथाऽऽवर्तो जलस्य च।
तदतद्भावरूपेयं तथा प्रकृतिरात्मनः।। ३०।।

kaṭaktvaṁ yathā hemno yathā'varto jalasya
tad-atad-bhāva-rupeyaṁ tathā prakṛtirātmanaḥ

कटकत्वं यथा हेम्नः *kaṭaktvaṁ yathā hemnaḥ= gold assumes the form of ornaments*
यथा *yathā= just as*
आवर्तः जलस्य च *āvartaḥ jalasya ca= water assumes the form of whirlpool*
तद् अतद् भावरूपा इयम् *tadatadbhāvarupeyaṁ = form of material body or sentient body*
तथा *tathā = similarly*
प्रकृतिर् आत्मनः *prakṛtir ātmanaḥ = nature of Brahma*

Just as gold assumes the form of ornaments and water assumes the shape of whirlpool. Similarly, by nature, Brahma assumes the forms of the material body or sentient body He pervades.

इदं हि जीवभूतात्म जडरूपमिदं भवेत्।
इत्यज्ञानात्मनो मोहो न च ज्ञानात्मनः क्वचिद्।। ३१।।

idaṁ hi jīvabhūtārma jaḍarūpamidaṁ bhavet
ityajñānātmano moho na ca jñānātmanaḥ kvacid

इदं हि *idaṁ hi = this is*

जीवभूतात्म *jīvabhūtārma = sentient body*

जडरूपम् इदं भवेत् *jaḍarūpamidaṁ bhavet = that is material body*

इति अज्ञान–आत्मनः मोहः *ityajñānātmanaḥ mohaḥ= this type of distinction is made by Ajñāni (a person devoid of proper and precise information of Ātmā and Paramātmā.*

न च ज्ञानात्मनः क्वचिद् *na ca jñānātmanaḥ kvacid= and not by Ātma Jñānī (a wise well informed of Ātmā and Paramātmā)*

One is sentient body, another is material body. This type of distinction is made by *Ajñānī* and not by *Ātma* Jñānī..

अज्ञस्य दुःखौघमयं ज्ञस्याऽऽनन्दमयं जगत् ।
अन्धं भुवनमन्धस्यप्रकाशं तु सचक्षुषः ।। ३२ ।।

ajñasya duḥkhaughamayaṁ jñasyānandamayaṁ jagat.
andhaṁ bhuvanam andhasya prakāśam tu sa-cakṣuṣaḥ

अज्ञस्य *ajñasya= for Ajñānī*

दुःखौघमयम् *duḥkh-aughamayam= full of sorrow*

ज्ञस्य *jñasya =for Jñānī (a person who has realized Ātmā and Paramātmā)*

आनन्दमयम् *ānandamayam= blissful*

जगत् *jagat= this world*

अन्धं भुवनम् अन्धस्य *andhaṁ bhuvanam andhasya= for blind, world is dark*

प्रकाशं तु सचक्षुषः *prakāśam tu sa-cakṣuṣaḥ= full of light for eye-sighted one*

For *Ajñānī*, this world is full of sorrow, but for *Jñānī* , the same is blissful. As for blind world is dark, while for eye-sighted one, it is full of light.

जगदेकात्मकं ज्ञस्य मूर्खस्याऽतीव दुःखदम् ।

शिशोरिव स्फुरद्यक्षा निशा पुंसस्तु केवला।।३३।।

jagad ekātmakaṁ jñasya mūrkhasyātīva duḥkhadam
śiśor iva sphurd yakṣā niśā punsastu kevalā.

जगद् *jagad= the world*
एकात्मकम् *ekātmakam=blissful*
ज्ञस्य *jñasya= for Ātma Jñānī*
मूर्खस्य *mūrkhasy= Ajñānī*
अतीव दुःखदम् *atīva duḥkhadam= utterly miserable*
शिशोरिव *śiśor iva=as to the child*
स्फुरत् यक्षा निशा *sphurd yakṣā niśā= night appears full of goblins and spectres*
पुंसस्तु केवला *punsastu kevalā= for grown ups and adults night is only night*

The world is blissful for *Jñānī*, but utterly miserable for *Ajñānī*, as the night appears full of goblins and specters to children and not to those of grown ups and adults.

अस्मिंन्ब्रह्मघटे नित्यमेकस्मिन्सर्वतः स्थिते।
न किंचिन्म्रियते नाम न च किंचन जीवति।।३४।।
यथोल्लासविलासेषु न नश्यति न जायते।। ३५।।

asmin brahma ghaṭe nityam ekasmin sarvataḥ sthite.
na kincinmriyate nāma na ca kincana jīvati
yathollāsavilāseṣu na naśyati na jāyate.

अस्मिन् ब्रह्मघटे *asmin brahma ghaṭe=in this universal pot of Brahma*
नित्यम् *nityam = eternal*
एकस्मिन् *ekasmin = unique*
सर्वतः स्थिते *sarvataḥ sthite= pervading whole world*
न किंचित् म्रियते नाम *na kincit mriyate nāma= nothing deems to*

perish

न च किंचन जीवति *na ca kincana jīvati= nothing deems to be born*

यथा *yathā= just as*

उल्लासविलासेषु *ullāsa-vilāseṣu= in merriness or wantonness*

न नश्यति न जायते *na naśyati na jāyate = neither is born nor perish*

In this universal pot of Brahma which is eternal, unique and pervading whole world, nothing deems to be born or perish. Just as nothing is born out of merriness or perish in wantonness.

तरंगादिमहाम्भोधौ भूतवृन्दं तथाऽऽत्मनि।
इदं नास्तीदमस्तीति भ्रान्तिर्नामाऽऽत्मनाऽऽत्मनि।। ३६।।

taraṅg-ādi mah-āmbhodhau bhūta-vṛndaṁ that-ātmani
idaṁ n-āstīdam-astīti bhrāntir nām-ātmanātmani.

तरंगादि–महाम्भोधौ *taraṅg-ādi mah-āmbhodhau= waves are located in vast expanse of ocean*

भूतवृन्दं तथा आत्मनि *bhūta-vṛndaṁ that-ātmani= similarly all beings are located in Paramātmā*

इदं नास्ति इदम् अस्ति *idaṁ nāstīdam-astīti= this exist and that not*

इति भ्रान्तिर् नाम *bhrāntir nāma = it is an illusion or mistake*

आत्मना *ātmanā= by us*

आत्मनि *ātmani =in Paramātmā*

All animate beings or inanimate things are located in the Paramātmā, as the waves in the vast expanse of the ocean. It is an illusion or mistake by us to think that this exists and that not.

शक्तिर्निर्हैतुकैवाऽन्तः स्फुरति स्फटिकांशुवत्।
जगच्छक्त्याऽऽत्मनाऽऽत्मैव ब्रह्म स्वात्मनि संस्थितम्।। ३७।।

śaktir-nirhaituk-aiv-āntaḥ sphurati sphaṭik-āñśuvat
jagac-chakty-ātman-ātmaiva brahma svātmani sansthitam.

शक्तिः *śaktir = power of creation*
निर्हैतुक *nirhaituka = without any external force/cause*
एव अन्तः स्फुरति *eva-āntaḥ sphurati = inborn power that reflects*
स्फटिकांशुवत् *sphaṭikāñśuvat = like the light of sphaṭika maṇi (crystal type gem)*
जगत् शक्त्या आत्मना *jagat śaktyā ātmanā = inborn power of creation of universe*
आत्मैव ब्रह्म *ātmaiva brahma = by Brahma Himself or by its own*
स्वात्मनि संस्थितम् *svātmani sansthitam = in Brahma*

Just as a light in sphaṭika maṇi shines in it by itself without any external force or cause, similarly there is inborn power of creation of universe in Brahma which reflects in Brahma by its own.

तरंगकणजालेन पयसीव पयो घनम् ।
शरीरनाशेनकथं ब्रह्मणो मृतधीर्भवेत् ।। ३८ ।।

taraṅga-kaṇa-jālena payasīva payo ghanam
śarīra-nāśena-kathaṁ brahmaṇo mṛta-dhīr-bhavet

तरंगकणजालेन *taraṅga-kaṇa-jālena = particles of water waves*
पयसीव पयो घनम् *payasīva payo ghanam = like add to the body of water in sea*
शरीरनाशेन *śarīra-nāśena = due to fall (death) of body*
कथं ब्रह्मणो मृतधीर्भवेत् *kathaṁ brahmaṇo mṛta-dhīr-bhavet = how can Ātmā be taken as dead ?*

As different particles of water waves fall into sea and add to the body of sea waters, so with the fall (death) of physical bodies, their Ātmā-s are added to Paramātmā. (Since the Ātmā-s of dead bodies merge with the Paramātmā upon their death). Thus with the death of physical body, how can Ātmā be taken as dead?

ब्रह्मणो व्यतिरिक्तं हि न शरीरादि विद्यते।
पयसो व्यतिरेकेण तरंगादि महार्णवे।। ३९।।

brahmaṇo vyatiriktaṁ hi śarīrādi vidyate
payaso vyatirekeṇa taraṅgādi mahārṇave

ब्रह्मणो व्यतिरिक्तम् *brahmaṇo vyatiriktam = without Ātmā*
हि न शरीरादि विद्यते *hi śarīrādi vidyate = as no physical body is possible (in ocean of Brahma)*
पयसो व्यतिरेकेण *payaso vyatirekeṇa= without water*
तरंगादि महार्णवे *taraṅgādi mahārṇave= no wave in ocean is possible*

As no wave is possible in ocean without waters, so no physical body is possible without Ātmā in the ocean of Paramātmā.

यः कणो या च कणिका या वीचिर्यस्तरंगकः।
यः फेनो या च लहरी तद्यथा वारि वारिणि।। ४०।।

yaḥ kaṇo yā ca kaṇikā yā vīcir yas-taraṅgakaḥ
yaḥ pheno yā ca laharī tadyathā vāri vāriṇi

यः कणः *yaḥ kaṇo= whatever particle*
या च कणिका *yā ca kaṇikā= whatever sub-prticle*
या वीचिः *yā vīciḥ = whatever wave*
यः तरंगकः *yas-taraṅgakaḥ= whatever current*
यः फेनः *yaḥ phenaḥ = whatever foam*
या च लहरी *yā ca laharī = whatever froth*
तद्यथा वारि वारिणि *tadyathā vāri vāriṇi = like they are all*

formations of water in water body

Whatever particle or sub-particle or wave or current or foam or froth in water is there, they are all different formations of waters in the water body.

यो देहो या च कलना यद्दृश्यं यौ क्षयाक्षयौ।
या च भावरचना योऽर्थस्तया तद्ब्रह्म ब्रह्मणि।।४१।।

yo deho yā ca kalanā yaddṛśyaṁ yau kṣayākṣayau
yā ca bhāvaracanā yo'rthastayā tadbrahma brahmaṇi

***यः देहः** yaḥ dehaḥ= body*
***या च कलना** yā ca kalanā=functions of sense organs*
***यद्दृश्यम्** yaddṛśyaṁ = enjoyable things or scenes*
***यौ क्षयाक्षयौ** yau kṣayākṣayau= all constructive or destructive ideas*
***या च भावरचना** yā ca bhāvaracanā= feelings*
***यः अर्थः** yaḥ arthaḥ = objectives of life*
***तया तद्ब्रह्म ब्रह्मणि** tayā tad brahma brahmaṇi=productions of embodied Ātmā (that remains confine to individual living body) in Paramātmā (that pervades whole living and non-living world).*

So, all bodies, functions of sense organs, enjoyable things or scenes, all constructive or destructive ideas, feelings, objectives of life are but productions of Ātmā in Parmātmā.

संस्थानरचना चित्रा ब्रह्मणः कनकादिव।
नान्यरूपा विमूढानां मृषैव द्वित्वभावना।। ४२।।

sansthāna-racanā citrā brahmaṇaḥ kanakādiva
nānyrūpā vimūḍhānāṁ mṛṣaiva dvitvabhāvanā

***संस्थानरचना** sansthāna-racanā= creation*
***चित्रा** citrā = various*

ब्रह्मण: *brahmaṇaḥ = of Brahma*
कनकादिव *kanakādiva = as ornaments are not distinct from gold*
नान्यरूपा *nānyrūpā=no oher form*
विमूढानां *vimūḍhānāṁ= of ignorant*
मृषैव *mṛṣaiva = erroneous*
द्वित्वभावना *dvitvabhāvanā= sense of duality i.e. effect (creation) is distinct from its cause or source*

Various creations of Paramātmā have no other form distinct from Him, as the various ornaments made of gold have no other form distinct from gold. (Effect or creation owes its properties to its cause/source). The sense of duality i.e. effect (creation) is distinct from its cause or source is the erroneous conception of *Ajñānī.*

Note: In context of *Yogavāsiṣtha, dvitav bhāvanā* means sense of duality i.e. creation is distinct from its cause or source. *Advait bhāvanā* means loss of sense of duality i.e. creation and cause are one and same and not different from each other.

मनो बुद्धिरहंकारस्तन्मात्राणीन्द्रयाणि च।
ब्रह्मैव सर्वं नानात्म सुखं दुःखं न विद्यते।। ४३।।

mano buddhir ahaṅkāras tanmātrāṇīndrayāṇi ca
brahmaiva sarvaṁ nānārma sukhaṁ duḥkhaṁ na vidyate.

मन: *manaḥ = manas (ability to desire, imagine)*
बुद्धि: *buddhir = buddhi (ability to decide, to conclude)*
अहंकार : *ahaṅkāraḥ = ahaṅkāra (ability of maintaining distinct identity or individuality)*
तन्मात्राणि *tanmātrāṇi= elementary sensations*
इन्द्रयाणि च *īndrayāṇi ca = sense organs*
ब्रह्मैव सर्वं *brahmaiva sarvam = all are various forms of embodied Ātmā*
नानात्म *nānārma= various forms*

सुखं दुःखं न विद्यते *sukhaṁ duḥkhaṁ na vidyate= pleasure and pain are not present*

Manas, buddhi, ahaṁkāra, five rudimentary/ elementary sensations (sound, skin sensation/touch, sight, taste, olfaction), five sensory organs (ears, eyes, nose, tongue and skin)-all are but various forms of Ātmā in the body. So, there should be no question of presence of pleasure and pain.

अयं सोऽहमिदं चित्तमित्याद्यर्थोत्थया गिरा।
शब्दप्रतिश्रवेणाऽद्राविवाऽऽत्माऽऽत्मनि जृम्भते।। ४४।।

ayaṁ so'hamidaṁ cittamityādyarthotthayā girā
śabdpratiśraveṇā'drāviv-ātmātmani jṛmbhate.

अयम् *ayaṁ= this*
सः *so = he/ she*
अहम् *aham =I*
इदम् *idam =that*
चित्तम् *cittam = citta (mind based awareness)*
इत्यादि अर्थः *ityādyarthaḥ = etc. significances*
उत्थया गिरा *utthayā girā = pronounced*
शब्दप्रतिश्रवेण *śabdpratiśraveṇa = echo or roaring cloud*
अद्राविव *adrāviva = in hilly terrain*
आत्मा आत्मनि जृम्भते *ātmātmani jṛmbhate = echo of Ātmā in Paramātmā*

The terms pronounced as he, she, I, this and that, and also the terms signifying *citta* (mind based awareness), are but the echo of Ātmā in Paramātmā, like the echo of roaring cloud in hilly terrain.

ब्रह्मैवाज्ञातज्ञत्वमभ्यागतमिव स्थितम्।
तथा हि दृश्यते स्वप्ने चेतसात्मात्मनात्मनः।। ४५।।

brahmaiv-ājñātajñatvam-abhyāgatamiva sthitam
tathā hi dṛśyate svapane cetasātmātmanātmanaḥ.

ब्रह्म एव *brahma eva = Brahma*
अज्ञात *ājñāta = unknown*
ज्ञत्वम् *jñatvam = worth knowing*
अभ्यागतम् इव स्थितम् *abhyāgatam iva sthitam = appears like stranger*
तथा हि *tathā hi = like*
दृश्यते *dṛśyate = seen*
स्वप्ने *svapane = in dream*
चेतसा आत्मा आत्मना *cetasā ātmā ātmanā= by our own citta*
आत्मनः *ātmanaḥ=our own images*

Brahma, which is worth knowing, appears unknown and stranger to us, due to our *ajñāna* (ignorance) of Him, like our own images seen by our own citta in a dream appear strange to us. (Our belief in the visible is the cause of our disbelief in the invisible Paramātmā and our familiarity with the objects of our waking state, makes us reject objects seen in dream as false).

अभावितं ब्रह्मतया ब्रह्माज्ञानमलं भवेत् ।
अभावितं हेमतया यथा हेम च मृद्भवेत् ।। ४६ ।।

abhāvitaṁ brahmatayā brahm-ājñāna-malaṁ bhavet
abhāvitaṁ hematayā yathā hema ca mṛd bhavet.

अभावितं ब्रह्मतया ब्रह्म *abhāvitaṁ brahmatayā brahma = Brahma (Paramātmā) not observed with the right notion of Brahma*
अज्ञानमलं भवेत् *ājñāna-malaṁ bhavet= reduces into a dirt of ajñāna*
अभावितं हेमतया यथा हेम *bhāvitaṁ hematayā yathā hema = as gold if not observed with the right notion of gold*
च मृद् भवेत *ca mṛd bhavet= reduces into a lump of clay*

Brahma (Paramātmā) not observed with the right notion of Brahma is reduced merely into a dirt of *ajñāna*, as gold if not observed with the right notion of gold is reduced merely into a lump of clay.

स्वयं प्रभुर्महात्मैव ब्रह्म बह्मविदो विदुः।
अपरिज्ञातमज्ञानमज्ञानामिति कथ्यते।। ४७।।

svayaṁ prabhur mahātmaiva brahma brahmavido viduḥ
aparijñātam-ajñānam-ajñānām-iti kathyate.

स्वयं प्रभु *svayaṁ prabhu= master of himself*
महात्मा इव *Mahātmā iva= supreme Ātmā*
ब्रह्म *brahma= Brahma (Paramātmā)*
बह्मविदो विदुः *brahmavido viduḥ= know by those who have realized Brahma*
अपरिज्ञातम् *aparijñātam= unknown*
अज्ञानम् *ajñānam= untraceable*
अज्ञानाम् इति कथ्यते *ajñānām-iti kathyate= said by those unable to realize Him*

Brahma (Paramātmā) is known as master of himself, Supreme Ātmā by those who have realized Him, but he is said to be unknown, untraceable, by those who are unable to realize Him.

ज्ञातं ब्रह्मतया ब्रह्म ब्रह्मैव भवति क्षणात्।
ज्ञातं हेमतया हेम हेमैव भवति क्षणात्।। ४८।।

Jñātaṁ brahmatayā brahma brahmaiva bhavati kṣaṇāt
Jñātaṁ hematayā hema hemaiva bhavati kṣaṇāt

ज्ञातं ब्रह्मतया ब्रह्म *Jñātaṁ brahmatayā brahma = Brahma (Paramātmā) when understood with the right notion of Brahma*
ब्रह्मैव भवति क्षणात् *brahmaiva bhavati kṣaṇāt= instantly assumes*

its real identity
ज्ञातं हेमतया हेम *Jñātaṁ hematayā hema= gold when recognized as gold*
हेमैव भवति क्षणात् *hemaiva bhavati kṣaṇāt=* instantly taken as such

Brahma (Paramātmā) when understood with the right notion of Brahma, instantly assumes its real identity, just as gold when recognized as gold instantly taken as such.

ब्रह्मात्मा सर्वशक्तिर्हि तद्यथा भावयत्पलम्।
निर्हेतुकः स्वयं शक्त्या तत्तथाशु प्रपश्यति।। ४६।।

brahm-ātmā sarva-śaktir-hi tadyathā bhāvayatpalam
nirhetukaḥ svayaṁ śaktyā tattath-āśu prapaśyati.

ब्रह्म आत्मा *brahma ātmā= one who has realized Brahma (Paramātmā)*
सर्वशक्तिर् हि *sarva-śaktir hi =all powerful*
तद्यथा भावयत् *tadyathā bhāvayat= whatever he desires*
पलम् *palam= instantly*
निर्हेतुकः *nirhetukaḥ=without any cause preceding it*
स्वयं शक्त्या *svayaṁ śaktyā=automatically*
तत् तथा आशु प्रपश्यति *tattath-āśu prapaśyati=the same materializes before him*

One who has realized Brahma (Paramātmā), becomes all powerful. Whatever he desires, materializes instantly before him automatically without any cause preceding it.

अकर्मकर्तृकरणमकारणमनामयम्।
स्वयं प्रभुं महात्मानं ब्रह्म ब्रह्मविदो विदुः।। ५०।।

akarma-kartṛ-karaṇam-akāraṇam-anāmayam
svayaṁ prabhuṁ mahātmānaṁ brahma brahmavido viduḥ

अकर्म *karma= free from the bondage of karma (willful action)*
कर्तृ *kartṛ= non-doer*
करणम् *karaṇam= need no driving force or aid of any type*
अकारणम् *akāraṇam= without cause*
अनामयम् *anāmayam= not vulnerable to actions*
स्वयं प्रभुम् *svayaṁ prabhuṁ=master of himself*
महात्मानम् *mahātmānaṁ= supreme Ātmā*
ब्रह्म ब्रह्मविदो विदुः *brahma brahmavido viduḥ= Brahma (Paramātmā) known to His seekers*

Brahma (Paramātmā) is known as the master of Himself, and supreme Ātmā by His seekers. He is free from the bondage of karmas, non-doer, without cause and needs no driving force and aid of any type. He is not vulnerable to afflictions.

अपरिज्ञातमज्ञानामज्ञानमिति कथ्यते ।
परिज्ञातं भवेज्ज्ञानमज्ञानपरिनाशनम् ।। ५१ ।।

aparijñātam ajñātam ajñānam iti kathyate
parijñātaṁ bhavej-jñānam ajñāna-parināśanam

अपरिज्ञातम् *aparijñātam= unknown*
अज्ञानाम् *ajñātam= ajñānī-s (uninformed)*
अज्ञानमिति कथ्यते *ajñānam iti kathyate=called ajñāna (lack of information)*
परिज्ञातम् *parijñātam=known*
भवेत् ज्ञानम् *bhavej-jñānam=called Jñāna (information)*
ज्ञानपरिनाशनम् *ajñāna-parināśanam=remover of ajñāna*

Till the time a thing remains unknown to uninformed, it is called *ajñāna*. As soon as it becomes known, It is called *Jñāna*, the remover of *ajñāna*.

बन्धुरेवापरिज्ञातो ह्यबन्धुरिति कथ्यते।
परिज्ञातो भवेद्बन्धुरबन्धुभ्रमनाशनात्।। ५२।।

bandhur-ev-āparijñāto hy-abandhur-iti kathyate
parijñāto bhaved bandhur-abandhu-bhrama nāśanāt

बन्धुर् एव *bandhur eva = friend*
अपरिज्ञातः *āparijñātaḥ = unrecognized*
हि अबन्धुर् इति कथ्यते *hi-abandhur-iti kathyate = known as a stranger*
परिज्ञातः भवेद् *parijñātaḥ bhaved = upon recognition, he becomes*
बन्धुर् *bandhur = a friend*
अबन्धु–भ्रमनाशनात् *abandhu-bhrama nāśanāt = confusion of strangeness is dispelled*

A friend when unrecognized is known as a stranger, but upon recognition he turns out to be a friend and confusion of strangeness is dispelled.

इदं त्वयुक्तमित्यन्तर्ज्ञाते सोदेति भावना।
यस्मादयुक्ताद्वैरस्याद्यया किल विरज्यते।। ५३।

idaṁ tvayuktam ityantar jñāte sodeti bhāvanā
yasmādayuktād vairasyād yayā kila virajyate

इदम *idam = Ātmā*
तु अयुक्तम् *tu ayuktam = not bound with body*
इति अन्तर्ज्ञाते *ityantar jñāte = when it is realized*
सोदेति भावना *sodeti bhāvanā = there develops Ātmajñāna*
यस्माद् अयुक्ताद् वैरस्यात् *yasmād ayuktād vairasyād = due to which one becomes detached (from worldly things) and develops distate towards body*
यया किल विरज्यते *yayā kila virajyate = resulting into renunciation*

When it is realized that the Ātmā is not bound with body, there develops *Ātmajñāna*, due to which one gets detached (from worldly things) and there develops distaste towards body resulting into renunciation.

द्वैतं त्वसत्यमित्यन्तर्ज्ञाते सोदेति भावना।
तस्माद्वैताच्च वैरस्याद्यया किल विरज्यते।। ५४।।

dvaitaṁ tvastayam-ityantarjñāte sodeti bhāvanā
tasmād-vaitācca vairasyad-yayā kila virajyate

द्वैतं तु असत्यम् *dvaitaṁ tu astayam= duality (company of body and Ātmā) is not permanent*
इति अन्तर्ज्ञाते *iti antarjñāte= when this reality is realized*
सोदेति भावना *sodeti bhāvanā= there develops Ātmajñāna*
तस्माद् वा एतात् च वैरस्यात् *tasmād-vā etāt ca vairasyāt= due to which develops a distate towards body*
यया किल विरज्यते *yayā kila virajyate= resulting into renunciation*

Duality (company of body and Ātmā) is not permanent, when this reality is realized, there develops *Ātmajñāna,* due to which develops a distate towards body resulting into renunciation.

अयं नाहमिति ज्ञाते स्फुटे सोदेति भावना ।
मिथ्याहंकारता तस्माद्यया नूनं विरज्यते।। ५५।।

ayaṁ nāham iti jñāte sphuṭe sodeti bhāvanā
mithyāhaṅkāratā tasmād-yayā nūnaṁ virajyate.

अयम् *ayam= this body*
न अहम् *na aham= I am not*
इति ज्ञाते स्फुटे *iti jñāte sphuṭe= when this is realized clearly*
सोदेति भावना *sodeti bhāvanā= Ātmajñāna emerges*
मिथ्या अहंकारता तस्मात् *mithyā ahaṅkāratā tasmāt= due to*

which feeling of false ahaṅkāra (distinct individual identity)
यया नूनं विरज्यते *yayā nūnaṁ virajyate= leading to renunciation (aversion towards worldy allurements)*

I am not the body, when this realty is clearly realized. There develops *Ātma jñāna,* due to which feeling of false *ahaṅkāra* gets dissolved leading to renunciation (aversion towards worldly allurements).

ब्रह्मैवाहमिति ज्ञाने सत्ये सोदेति भावना।
तस्मिन्सत्ये निजे रूपे यथान्तः परिलीयते।
सति विस्तारजे तस्मिन्ब्रह्मेदमिति वेद्म्यहम्।।५६।।

brahmaiv-aham iti jñāne satye sodeti bhāvanā
tasmin satye nije rupe yathāntaḥ parilīyate
sati vistāraje tasmin brahmedam iti vedmyaham

ब्रह्म एव अहम् *brahma eva aham= I am Ātmā*
इति ज्ञाने सत्ये *iti jñāne satye= when this truth is realized*
सा उदेति भावना *sodeti bhāvanā= Ātma Jñāna rises*
तस्मिन् सत्ये निजे रूपे *tasmin satye nije rupe = when this truth is realized (due to which) he (seeker) himself*
यथा अन्तः परिलीयते *yathā antaḥ parilīyate= gets absorbed in his Ātmā*
सति विस्तारजे तस्मिन् *sati vistāraje tasmin=upon merging with Paramātmā, Ātmā gets expanded*
ब्रह्म इदम् इति वेद्मि अहम् *brahma idam iti vedmi-aham= as a seeker, I realize Brahma (Paramātmā)*

I am not the body but pure Ātmā, when this truth is realized, there arises *Ātmajñāna.* As such the seeker gets absorbed in his/her own true Ātmā and association of Ātmā with body gets disengaged. Ātmā gets expanded when it merges with Paramātmā (universal self). (This process is known as universalization of individuated Ātmā). Consequent upon which, I, as a seeker, realize true nature of Brahma (Paramātmā).

त्वमहंत्वादिबाधे तत्सदित्यादि जगद्गतम्।
सत्यं सर्वप्रकाराढ्यं ब्रह्मेदमिति वेद्म्यहम्।। ५७।।

tvam-ahaṁtvādi-bādhe tatsad-ityādi jagad gatam
satyaṁ sarva-prakārāḍhyaṁ brahmedam iti vedmy-aham

त्वं अहंत्वादिबाधे *tvam-ahaṁtvādi-bādhe= when notion of ahaṅkāra (distinct individual identity) ceases to occur*
तत्सत् इत्यादि *tatsat ityādi= truthfulness of Paramātmā (Brahma) is revealed*
जगद्गतम् सत्यं सर्वप्रकाराढ्यम् *jagad-gatam satyaṁ sarva-prakārāḍhyaṁ= true nature (mithyātva i.e.perishability) of world gets busted by all means*
ब्रह्म इदम् इति वेद्मि अहम् *brahma idam iti vedmi-aham= I visualize Brahma (Paramātmā)*

When notion of ahaṅkāra ceases to occur, truthfulness of Paramātmā is revealed and true nature (perishability) of world gets busted by all means and I, as a seeker, visualize Brahma (Paramātmā).

न मे दुःखं न कर्माणि न मे मोहो न वांछितम्।
समः स्वस्थो विशोकोऽस्मि ब्रह्माहमिति सत्यता।। ५८।।

na me duḥkhaṁ na karmāṇi na me moho na vāñchitam
samaḥ svastho viśoko'smi brahma-aham iti satyatā

न मे दुःखम् *na me duḥkham= I am not afflicted by sorrows*
न कर्माणि *na karmāṇi= set free from the responsibilities of my duties*
न मे मोहो *na me mohair= free from attachments*
न वांछितम् *na vāñchitam= free from desires*

समः स्वस्थः *samaḥ svasthaḥ= maintain balance, become self settled*
विशोकः अस्मि *viśokaḥ asmi= free from grief*
ब्रह्म अहम् इति सत्यता *brahma-aham iti satiate= I am only Ātmā and not body, when this truth is realized*

I am only Ātmā and not body, when this truth is realized, I am not afflicted by sorrows, set free from the responsibilities of my duties, attachments and desires, maintain balance, become self settled and free from afflictions.

कलाकलंकमुक्तोऽस्मि सर्वमस्मि निरामयः।
न त्यजामि न वांछामि ब्रह्माहमिति सत्यता।। ५९।।

kalākalaṅk-mikto'smi sarvam-asmi nirāmayaḥ
na tyajāmi na vāñchāmi brahm-āham iti satyatā

कलाकलंकमुक्तः अस्मि *kalākalaṅk-miktaḥ asmi=become indifference to praise and blame*
सर्वमस्मि निरामयः *sarvam-asmi nirāmayaḥ=free from afflictions*
न त्यजामि *na tyajāmi= neither I abandon a thing disliked by me*
न वांछामि *na vāñchāmi= nor do I desire to gain things that I like*
ब्रह्म अहम् इति सत्यता *brahma-aham iti satiate= I am only Ātmā and not body, when this truth is revealed*

Upon the revealation of truth that I am only Ātmā and not body, I become indifference to praise and blame, free from afflictions. I don't want to have choice between likes and dislikes.

अहं रक्तमहं मांसमहमस्थीन्यहं वपुः।
चिदहं चेतनं चाहं ब्रह्माहमिति सत्यता।।६०।।

ahaṁ raktaṁ ahaṁ mānsam aham asthīni ahaṁ vapuḥ
cidaṁ cetanaṁ cāhaṁ brahm-āham iti satyatā

अहं रक्तम् ahaṁ raktaṁ = blood
अहं मांसम् ahaṁ mānsam = flesh
अहम् अस्थीनि aham asthīni = bones
अहं वपुः ahaṁ vapuḥ = skin
चिद् अहम् cidaṁ = bio-electric current
चेतनं च अहम् cetanaṁ cāhaṁ = intelligence
ब्रह्म अहम् इति सत्यता brahm-āham iti satiate = I am only Ātmā and not body, when this truth is revealed

Upon attainment of Ātmajñāna, I find my blood, flesh, bones, skin, bio-electric current and intelligence fused with Ātmā and not separate ones.

द्यौरहं खमहं सार्कमहमाशा भुवोऽप्यहम्।
अहं घटपटाकारो ब्रह्माहमिति सत्यता।।६१।।

dyaur ahaṁ kham-ahaṁ sārkam aham āśā bhuvo'pyaham
ahaṁ ghaṭa-paṭākāro brahmāham-iti satyatā

द्यौर् अहम् dyaur aham = I find myself merge with celestial sphere
खम् अहम् सार्कम् अहम् khaṁ aham sārkaṁ aham = I merge with sky and its luminaries
आशा भुवः अपि अहम् āśā bhuvaḥ api aham = I merge with different quarters of earth
अहं घटपटाकारः ahaṁ ghaṭa-paṭākāraḥ = I merge with designs of pots and clothes
ब्रह्म अहम् इति सत्यता brahma aham-iti satiate = Upon attainment of Ātmajñāna

Upon attainment of Ātmajñāna, I find myself merged with celestial sphere, sky and its luminaries, different quarters of earth, designs of pots and clothes.

अहं तृणमहं चोर्वी गुल्मोऽहं काननाद्यहम्।
शैलसागरसार्थोऽहं ब्रह्मैकत्वं किल स्थितम्।।६२।।

ahaṁ tṛṇam ahaṁ corvī gulmo'haṁ kānan-ādyaham
śaila-sāgara-sārtho'haṁ brahmaiktvṁ kila sthitam

अहं तृणम् *ahaṁ tṛṇam =I get connected with grass*
अहं च उर्वी *ahaṁ ca urvī= I get connected with soil*
गुल्मः अहम् *gulmaḥ ahaṁ= I get connected with bush*
काननादि अहम् *kānan-ādi aham= I get connected with forest, etc.*
शैलसागरसार्थः अहम् *śaila-sāgara-sārthaḥ aham= I get connected with hill, ocean and all other living beings*
ब्रह्मैकत्वं किल स्थितम् *brahmaiktvṁ kila sthitam= When I become one with Paramātmā, (upon attaining Ātma jñāna)*

When I become one with Paramātmā, I get connected with grass, soil, bush, forest etc., hill, ocean, and all living beings.

आदानदानसंकोचपूर्विका भूतशक्तयः।
सर्वमेव चिदात्मास्मि ब्रह्मण्याततरूपधृक्।। ६३।।

ādāna-dāna-saṅkoca-pūrvikā bhūtaśaktayaḥ
sarvam eva cid-ātmāsmi brahmaṇyātata-rūpa-dhṛk

आदान–दान–संकोच–पूर्विका *ādāna-dāna-saṅkoca-pūrvikā= functions like reception, emission, and contraction*
भूतशक्तयः *bhūtaśaktayaḥ= material bodies*
सर्वम् एव *sarvam eva = All these functions*
चिद् आत्मा अस्मि *cid-ātmā-asmi= me as Ātmā inheriting bio-electric current*
ब्रह्मणि आततरूपधृक् *brahmaṇi ātata-rūpa-dhṛk= exist boldly in Brahma (Paramātmā) in their extended forms*

Even the functions like reception, emission, and contraction in material bodies and me as cidātmā (bio-electric current or intelligence) assumes their universal forms in Brahma (Paramātmā).

NB: Since inanimate and animate bodies have a lmited jurisdiction, but Paramātmā has unlimited jurisdiction, when a particular quality transfer from individual object or being to Paramātmā, its scope gets automatically extended.

लतागुल्मांकुरादीनामहंसंभवनैषिणाम् ।
चिदात्मान्तर्गतं शान्तं परं ब्रह्म रसात्मकम् ।।६४।।

latā-gulm-aṅkur-ādīnām-ahaṁ sambhav-ainiṣinām
cid-ātmāntargataṁ śāntaṁ paraṁ brahma rasātmakam

लतागुल्मांकुरादीनाम् *latā-gulm-aṅkur-ādīnām= of creepers, plants and sprouts*
अहं *ahaṁ= I am*
संभवना ईषिणाम् *sambhavanā īṣinām= hastened growth*
चिदात्मा *cid-ātmā=an intelligent Ātmā*
अन्तर्गतम् *ntargatam= exist in*
शान्तम् *śāntam= serene*
परं ब्रह्म रसात्मकम् *paraṁ brahma rasātmakam=Paramātmā who is full of rasa (life force of universal creation)*

I am also an intelligent Ātmā that exist in Paramātmā who is of serene nature and full of rasa (life force of universal creation) and hastens the growth of of creepers, plants and sprouts.

यस्मिन्सर्वं यतः सर्वं यत्सर्वं सर्वतश्च यत् ।
यो मतः सर्व एकात्मा परं ब्रह्मेति निश्चयः।। ६५।।

yasmin sarvaṁ yataḥ sarvaṁ yatsarvaṁ sarvataśca yat
yo mataḥ sarva ekātmā paraṁ brahmeti niścayaḥ

यस्मिन् सर्वम् *yasmin sarvaṁ=who is the abode of everything*
यतः सर्वम् *yataḥ sarvaṁ=who is the cause of everything*
यत् सर्वम् *yatsarvaṁ=who is all in all*
सर्वतश्च यत् *sarvataśca yat=who is all pervading*
यो मतः सर्व एकात्मा *yo mataḥ sarva ekātmā= who is regarded as one Ātmā for all Ātmā-s*
परं ब्रह्म इति निश्चयः *paraṁ brahma iti niścayaḥ= He should be ascertained as Paraṁ Brahma (Supreme Brahma/Paramātmā)*

Here the nature of Paraṁ Paramātmā is described. Para Brahma (Paramātmā) is one who is the abode of everything, who is the cause of every thing, who is all in all, who is all pervading, and who is regarded as one Ātmā for all Ātmā-s, He should be ascertained as Paraṁ Brahma (Paraṁ Paramātmā).

चिदात्मा ब्रह्म सत्सत्यमृतं ज्ञ इति नामभिः।
प्रोच्यते सर्वगं तत्त्वं चिन्मात्रं चेत्यवर्जितम्।। ६६।।

cidātmā brahma satsatyam amṛtaṁ jña iti nāmabhiḥ
procyate sarvagaṁ tattvaṁ cin-mātraṁ cetya-varjitam

चिदात्मा ब्रह्म *cidātmā brahma=Brahma (Paramātmā) is pure intelligence*
सत् सत्यम् ऋतं ज्ञ इति नामभिः प्रोच्यते *sat-satyam-ṛtaṁ jña iti nāmabhiḥ procyate=* called by name of Sat (eternal), Satya (truth), Ṛta (source of inner laws sustaining universal creation) and Jña (all knowing).
सर्वगम् *sarvagaṁ= all pervading*
तत्त्वम् *tattvaṁ = basic essence of universal creation*
चिन्मात्रम् *cin-mātram= all conscious*
चेत्य–वर्जितम् *cetya-varjitam =imperceptible*

Brahma (Paramātmā) is Cid Ātmā (Pure Ātmā). He is called by name of Sat (eternal), Satya (truth), Ṛta (source of inner laws sustaining universal creation) and Jña (all knowing). He is all pervading, basic essence of universal creation, all conscious and imperceptible.

आभासमात्रममलं सर्वभूतात्मबोधकम् ।
सर्वत्रावस्थितं शान्तं चिद्ब्रह्मेत्यनुभूयते ।। ६७ ।।

ābhās-mātram amalaṁ sarva-bhūtātma-bodhakaṁ
sarvatrāvasthitaṁ śāntaṁ cidbrahmetyanubhūyate

आभासमात्रम् *ābhās-mātram = one can have only an inkling of Him*
अमलम् *amalam = pure*
सर्वभूतात्म–बोधकम् *sarva-bhūtātma-bodhakam = makes Ātmā-s of all living beings known*
सर्वत्र अवस्थितम् *sarvatra avasthitam = omnipresent*
शान्तम् *śāntam = serene or undisturbed*
चिद्ब्रह्म इति अनुभूयते *cid brahma iti anubhūyate = Cid Brahma (Pure Paramātmā) is realized*

Seekers realize Cid Brahma (Paramātmā) as pure, one can have only an inkling of Him. He makes Ātmā-s of all living beings known. He is Omnipresent and always remains undisturbed.

मनोबुद्धीन्द्रियव्रातसमस्तकलनान्वितम् ।
भेदं त्यक्त्वा स्वमाभासं चिद्ब्रह्माहमनामयम् ।। ६८ ।।

mano-buddhīndriyavrāta samasta-kalanānvitam
bhedaṁ tyaktvā svamābhāsaṁ cid-brahmāham-anāmayam

मनः *manaḥ = manas (ability to think, desire and imagine)*
बुद्धि *buddhi = buddhi (ability to decide, to conclude)*
इन्द्रियव्रात *indriya-vrāta = sense organs*
समस्तकलनान्वितम् *samasta-kalanānvitam = their all functions*

***भेदं त्यक्त्वा** bhedaṁ tyaktvā= distinction is dispelled*
***स्वमाभासम्** svamābhāsam= realization of true nature*
***चिद्ब्रह्म अहम्** cid-brahma aham= I am Pure Ātmā*
***अनामयम्** -anāmayam= free from afflictions*

The distinction between manas, buddhi, sense organs and their functions is dispelled and the seeker is able to realize his true nature that He is pure Ātma free from afflictions.

शब्दादीनामशेषाणां कारणानां जगत्स्थितेः।
तत्त्वावकाशकं स्वच्छं चिद्ब्रह्मास्ति न मे क्षयः।। ६९।।

śabd-ādīnām-aśeṣāṇāṁ kāraṇānāṁ jagatshiteḥ
tattvāvakāśakaṁ svacchaṁ cidbrahmāsti na me kṣayaḥ

***शब्दादीनाम् अशेषाणाम्** śabd-ādīnām-aśeṣāṇām=sound etc. five primary sensations are*
***कारणानां** kāraṇānāṁ = the cause of*
***जगत्स्थितेः** jagatshiteḥ= sustenance of universe*
***तत्त्व अवकाशकम्** tattva avakāśakam= manifestor of all these elements*
***स्वच्छम्** svaccham= pure*
***चिद्ब्रह्म अस्ति** cidbrahma asti = is Cid Brahma*
***न मे क्षयः** na me kṣayaḥ = embodied Ātmā-s don't get perished in this process of manifestation.*

Five elementary sensations of sound, touch, sight, taste, and smell are the cause of sustenance of universe. Pure Cid Brahma (Paramātmā) is the manifestor of these five elementary sensations. Embodied Ātmā-s don't get perished in this process of manifestation.

अनारतगलत्स्वच्छचिद्धारागहनात्मकम्।
आलोकः सुमनोमौनं चिद्ब्रह्मास्त्यमृतं परम्।। ७०।।

anārata-galat-svaccha-ciddhārāgahanātmakam
ālokaḥ sumanomaunaṁ cidbrahmāstyamṛtaṁ param

अनारत *anārata= continuously*
गलत् *galat= flows*
स्वच्छ–चिद् धारा *svaccha-cid-dhārā=pure electric current*
गहनात्मकम् *gahanātmakam= impenetrable*
आलोकः सुमनोमौनं *ālokaḥ sumanomaunam= visualization is charming and undescribable*
चिद्ब्रह्म अस्ति *cidbrahma asti = embodied Brahma is*
अमृतं परम् *amṛtaṁ param= supreme immortal*

Impenetrable pure electric current of embodied Brahma (Paramātmā) flows continuously in the universe. His visualization is charming and indescribable in words. Embodied Brahma is supreme immortal.

अनारतगलद्रूपं नित्यं चानुभवामृतम्।
अहं निःशेषचक्राणि चिद्ब्रह्माहमलेपकम्।।७१।।

anāratagaladrūpaṁ nityaṁ cānubhav-āmṛtam
ahaṁ niḥśeṣacakrāṇi cidbrahmāham-alepkam

अनारत *anārat= continuous*
गलत् *galad=flow*
रूपम् *rūpam= nature*
नित्यम् *nityam=permanent*
च अनुभव–अमृतम् *ca anubhava-amṛtam=realization is immortalizing*
अहं निःशेषचक्राणि *ahaṁ niḥśeṣacakrāṇi= all dominions of ahaṅkāra*
चिद्ब्रह्म *cid brahma=embodied Brahma*
अहम् *aham= I*

अलेपकम् *alepkam= liberating*

Continuous flow is the permanent nature of Embodied Brahma (Paramāmā). His realization is immortalizing and liberates the seekers like me from all dominions of *ahaṅkāra*.

सुषुप्तसदृशं शान्तमालोकविमलात्मकम्।
संभोगोत्तममाभासं चिद्ब्रह्मास्त्यपवासनम्।। ७२।।

suṣupta-sadṛśaṁ śāntam-āloka-vimalātmakam
saṁbhogottamam-ābhāsaṁ cid-brahm-āstyapavāsanam

सुषुप्तसदृशम् *suṣupta-sadṛśam=like deep sleep*
शान्तम् *śāntam=quietness*
आलोक–विमलात्मकम् *āloka-vimalātmakam=full of pure divine light*
संभोगोत्तमम् आभासम् *saṁbhogottamam-ābhāsam=feels greater delight than that of orgasm followed by sexual discourse*
चिद्ब्रह्म अस्ति *cid-brahma-asti= Realization of embodied Brahma (Paramātmā)*
अपवासनम् *apavāsanam= purging of all vāsanās (impressions of will full acions/karmas imprinted unconsciously in mind).*

Realization of Embodied Brahma is full of pure divine light and quietness and calmness of deep sleep. The seeker feels greater delight than that of orgasm followed by sexual discourse and is purged of all *vāsanās* (impressions of karmas imprinted unconsciously on mind).

खण्डादिस्वादुसंवित्तिरीषन्मात्रा तु तिष्ठति।
चित्तादिष्ववबद्धेषु तद्धि ब्रह्माहमच्युतः।।७३।।

khaṇḍādi svādusaṁvittir-īṣan-mātrā tu tiṣṭhati
cittādiṣvavbaddheṣu taddhi brahmāham-acyutaḥ

खण्डादि–स्वादु–संवित्तिर् *khaṇḍādi svādu-saṁvittir=sweet taste of candied sugar*
ईषन्मात्रा तु तिष्ठति *īṣan-mātrā tu tiṣṭhati= is short lived*
चित्तादिषु अवबद्धेषु *cittādiṣu avbaddheṣu= due to perceiving limitations of sense organs*
तद्धि ब्रह्म अहम् *taddhi brahma aham=when I realize Brahma that is*
अच्युतः *acyutaḥ= permanent*

The sweet taste of candied sugar is shortlived, due to the perceiving limitation of the sense organ, whereas, Brahma jñāna (realization of Brahma) is a permanent phenomenon, because it is attained upon victory over the senses.

कान्तासंसक्तचित्तस्य चन्द्रे समुदिते सति।
चन्द्रप्रत्ययसत्वात्म चिद्ब्रह्माहमनामयम्।। ७४।।

kāntā-sansakta-cittasya candre samudite sati
candra-pratyaya-satvātma cid-brahm-āham-anāmayam

कान्ता–संसक्त–चित्तस्य kāntā-sansakta-cittasya= *One whose mind is possessed with his beloved*
चन्द्रे समुदिते सति *candre samudite sati=on the rise of moon*
चन्द्र–प्रत्यय–सत्वात्म candra-pratyaya-satvātma= *beholds his beloved's bright countenance identic with the shining orb of the moon*
चिद्ब्रह्म अहम् *cid-brahm-āham=* when Intelligent Brahma is realized by me
अनामयम् *anāmayam= become immune to afflictions*

One whose mind is possessed with his beloved, beholds her bright countenance identic with the shining orb of the moon, upon its rise. Similarly, when embodied Brahma is realized by me, I find myself as identic with Brahma, and become immune of afflictions.

भूमिष्ठनरदृष्टीनां लग्नानां खे निशाकरे।
या खस्था ननु चिच्छक्तिस्तच्चिद्ब्रह्मास्ति निर्मलम्।। ७५।।

bhūmiṣṭha-nara-dṛṣṭīnāṁ lagnānāṁ khe niśākare
yā khasthā nanu cicchaktis-taccid-brahm-āsti nirmalam

भूमिष्ठनरदृष्टीनाम् *bhūmiṣṭha-nara-dṛṣṭīnām= When people standing on earth fix their gaze*
लग्नानां खे निशाकरे *lagnānāṁ khe niśākare= on the moon positioned in sky*
या खस्था ननु चित् शक्तिः *yā khasthā nanu cit śaktiḥ = their sky centred power of vision*
तत् चिद्ब्रह्म अस्ति निर्मलम् *taccid-brahma-asti nirmalam=that of pure Ātmā*

When people standing on earth fix their gaze on the moon positioned in sky, their sky centered power of vision is nothing but that of pure Ātmā.

सुखदुःखादिकलनाविकलो निर्मलस्तथा।
सत्यानुभवरूपात्म चिद्ब्रह्मात्मास्मि शाश्वतः।। ७६।।
sukha-duḥkhādi-kalanā-vikalo- nirmalas-tathā
satyānubhavarūpātma cid-brahm-ātm-āsmi śāśvataḥ

सुखदुःखादिकलनाविकलो *sukha-duḥkhādi-kalanā-vikalo= immune of the feelings of pain and pleasure*
निर्मलस्तथा *nirmalas-tathā= stainless*
सत्य–अनुभवरूपात्म *satyānubhavarūpātma= realization in true sense*
चिद्ब्रह्म अत्मास्मि *cid-brahm-ātm-āsmi=when I realized pure Brahma*
शाश्वतः *śāśvataḥ=eternal*

When I realized eternal embodied Brahma, which is a realization in true sense, I became stainless and immune of the feelings of pain and pleasure.

Hereunder is explained the nature of seeker who has realized Brahma/Ātmā.

असंस्तुताध्वगालोके मनस्यन्यत्र संस्थिते।
या प्रतीतिरनागस्का तच्चिदब्रह्मास्मि सर्वगः।। ७७।।

asanstut-ādhvagā-loke mansyanyatra-sansthite
yā pratītir-anāgaskā taccid-brahm-āsmi sarvagaḥ

असंस्तुत–अध्वगा लोके *asanstut-ādhvagā-loke = In the mundane world, as a traveler while proceeding on an unknown path*
मनसि अन्यत्र संस्थिते *mansi anyatra-sansthite = manas being preoccupied with thoughts*
या प्रतीतिर् अनागस्का *yā pratītir-anāgaskā = remains aloof of midway objects*
तत् चिद्ब्रह्म अस्मि सर्वगः *tat cid-brahma-asmi sarvagaḥ = so is the nature of a seeker who has realized all pervading embodied Brahma*

As a traveler, preoccupied with thoughts, remains aloof of midway objects while proceeding on an unknown path, so is the nature of a seeker who has realized all pervading embodied Brahma. He remains aloof of worldly objects when meged in Him.

भूर्वायवनिलबीजानां संबन्धेऽङ्कुरकर्मसु।
शक्तिरुद्गमनीयान्तस्तच्चिद्ब्रह्माहमाततम्।। ७८।।

bhūr-vāyav-anila-bijānāṁ saṁbandhe'ṅkura-karmasu
śaktir-udgamanīyāntas-taccid-brahm-āham-ātatam

भूर्–वायु–अनिल–बीजानां संबन्धे *bhūr-vāyu-anila-bijānāṁ saṁbandhe = when mud, water, air and seed are amalgamated*

अङ्कुर कर्मसु *ṅkura-karmasu= process of germination takes place*

शक्तिर् उद्गमनीया अन्तः *śaktir-udgamanīyā antaḥ= sprouting process in seed*

तत् चिद्ब्रह्म *taccid-brahma = that is due to presence of embodied Brahma in seeds*

अहम् आततम *-āham-ātatam= I am also pervavded by Him*

With the amalgamation of mud, water, air and seed, the process of germination takes place. The sprouting process takes place due to presence of embodied Brahma in a seed. I am also pervaded by Him

खर्जूरनिम्बबिम्बानां स्वयमात्मनि तिष्ठताम्।
या स्वादसत्ता लीनान्तस्तद्ब्रह्म चिदहं समः।। ७६।।

kharjur-nimba-bimbānāṁ svayam-ātmani tiṣṭhatām
yā svād-sattā līnāntas-tad-brahma cidahaṁ samaḥ

खर्जूरनिम्बबिम्बानाम् kharjur-nimba-bimbānām=of the *fruits of date, neem and bimb (Momordica monadelpha- botanical name) etc.*

स्वयम् अत्मनि तिष्ठताम् या स्वादसत्ता *svayam-ātmani tiṣṭ hatām=whatever inherent taste*

लीना अन्तः yā svād-sattā līnāntas= is concealed in them

तद् ब्रह्म tad-brahma = that is due to the presence of Brahma

चिद् अहं समः cid ahaṁ samaḥ= He is like Cid Ātmā (embodied Ātmā) in them

The inherent tastes of fruit of date, neem and bimb (Momordica monadelpha- botanical name) etc. concealed in them are due to the presence of Brahma in them. He acts like that of embodied Ātmā in them

खेदानन्दविमुक्तान्तः संवित्तिर्मननोदया।
लाभालाभविधौ तुल्या चिद्ब्रह्मास्मि निरामयम्।। ८०।।

khed-ānand-vimuktāntaḥ saṁvittir-mananodayā
lābha-alābha-vidhau tulyā cid-brahm-āsmi nirāmayam

खेद आनन्द–विमुक्त *kheda-ānand-vimukta= become free from pleasure and pain*
अन्तः संवित्तिर् मननोदया *antaḥ saṁvittir-mananodayā= I developed such an internal perception and thinking*
लाभ अलाभविधौ तुल्या *lābha-alābha-vidhau tulyā= maintain equipoise in the matter of profit or loss*
चिद् ब्रह्म अस्मि *cid-brahma-asmi= I realize embodied Brahma (Paramātmā pervading the body of animate beings or inanimate things)*
निरामयम् *nirāmayam=free from afflictions*

When I realize embodied Brahma, I developed such an internal perception and thinking that liberates me from the feeling of the pain and pleasure. I maintain equipoise in the matter of profit or loss and become free from afflictions.

यावद् भूम्यर्कमेतावद्दृष्टि सूत्रं यदाततम्।
तन्मध्यसदृशं शान्तं निर्मलं चिदहं ततम्।। ८१।।

yāvad bhūmyarkam-etāvaddṛṣṭi sūtraṁ yadātatam
tanmadhya-sadṛśaṁ śāntaṁ nirmalaṁ cidahaṁ tatam

यावद् *yāvad=as long as*
भूमि अर्कम् *bhūmi-arkam=between earth and sun*
एतावद् दृष्टि सूत्रं यदाततम् *etāvaddṛṣṭi sūtraṁ yadātatam=expanse of visible space*
तन्मध्यसदृशम् *tanmadhya-sadṛśaṁ= that space*
शान्तम् śāntaṁ=compose
निर्मलम् nirmalaṁ= pure

चिदहं ततम् *cidahaṁ tatam=pervaded by embodied Brahma (Paramātmā)*

As long as expanse of visible space is there between earth and sun, it is also pervaded by pure and compose embodied Brahma (Paramātmā pervading universe).

जाग्रत्यपि सुषुप्तेऽपि तत्स्वप्नेऽपि तथोदितम्।
तुर्यं रूपमनाद्यन्तं चिद्ब्रह्माहमनामयम्।। ८२।।

jāgratyapi suṣupte'pi tatsvapne'pi tathoditam
turyaṁ rūpam-anādyantaṁ cidbrahm-āham-anāmayam

जाग्रति अपि *jāgrati api = even while waking*
सुषुप्ते अपि *suṣupte api= sleeping*
तत्स्वप्ने अपि *tat svapne api =dreaming*
तथा उदितम् *tathā uditam = upon the rise of sense of self awareness*
तुर्यं रूपम् *turyaṁ rūpam=turya state*
अनाद्यन्तं *anādyantam=without beginning or end*
चिद्ब्रह्म अहम् अनामयम् *cidbrahma-aham-anāmayam= embodied Ātmā free from sufferings*

While passing through the states of waking, sleeping and dreaming one remains aware of one's existence. Upon Ātmajñāna, I enter the turīya state where I become embodied Ātmā without beginning or end and free from sufferings.

पुंसां क्षेत्रशतोत्थानामिक्षूणां स्वादुवत्स्थितम्।
सर्वेषामेकरूपं तच्चिद्ब्रह्मास्ति समः स्थितः।। ८३।।

punsāṁ kṣetra-śatotthānām-ikṣuṇāṁ svāduvat-sthitam
sarveṣām-ekarūpaṁ taccid-brahm-āsmi samaḥ sthitaḥ

पुंसाम् *punsām= all human beings*

क्षेत्रशत–उत्थानाम् *kṣetra-śatot-uOthānām = planted and grown in hundreds of different fields*

इक्षूणां स्वादुवत् स्थितम् *ikṣuṇāṁ svāduvat-sthitam = sweetness present in sugar canes*

सर्वेषाम् *arveṣām = in all*

एकरूपम् *sekarūpam = same*

तत् चिद्ब्रह्म अस्ति समः स्थितः *taccid-brahma-asti samaḥ sthitaḥ = similarly embodied Brahma is present equally in all beings and things*

As the same sweetness is present in the sugar canes even though planted and grown in hundreds of different fields, similarly embodied Brahma is present equally in all beings and things across the world.

सर्वगा प्रकृता स्वच्छरूपा भानोरिव प्रभा ।
आलोककारिणी कान्ता चिद्ब्रह्मेदमहं ततम् ।। ८४ ।।

sarvagā prakṛtā svaccharūpā bhānoriva prabhā
āloka-kāriṇī kāntā cidbrahmedam-ahaṁ tatam

सर्वगा *sarvagā = all pervading*

प्रकृता *prakṛtā = natural*

स्वच्छरूपा *svaccharūpā = purified*

भानोर् इव प्रभा *bhānoriva prabhā = like illumination of sun*

आलोककारिणी *āloka-kāriṇī = illuminating*

कान्ता *kāntā = splendour*

चिद्ब्रह्म इदम् अहं ततम् *cidbrahmedam-ahaṁ tatam = embodied Brahma pervades this world as its inner being*

Like all pervading, natural, and purified sun-shine illuminates the whole solar system, similarly illuminting splendour of embodied Brahma pervades the whole world as its inner being.

संभोगानन्दलववदमृतास्वादशक्तिवत्।
स्वानुभूत्यैकमात्रं यच्चिद्ब्रह्माास्मि तदव्ययम्।। ८५।।

sambhog-ānanda-lava-vad-amṛt-asvād-śakti-vat
svānubhūty-aik-mātraṁ yaccid-brahm-āsmi-tadavyayam

संभोग–आनन्द–लववद् sambhog-ānanda-lava-vad= sexual orgasm
अमृत–आस्वाद–शक्तिवत् *amṛt-asvād-śakti-vat=like the taste of nectre*
स्वानुभूति एकमात्रम् svānubhūty-aik-mātram=self enjoyable only
यत् चिद्ब्रह्म अस्मि तदव्ययम् *yaccid-brahma-asmi-tadavyayam=*
Realization of embodied Brahma attained by me is inexhaustible

Realization of embodied Brahma attained by me is inexhaustible. Its ecstatic experience is enjoyable by the seeker alone, like the sexual orgasm and taste of nectre is cherished only by those who happended to enjoy them.

प्रोतांगमपि गुप्तास्यं देहे तन्तुर्बिसे यथा।
छेदे भेदे स्फुरद्रूपं चिद्ब्रह्माहमनामयम्।। ८६।।

protāṅgam-api guptāsyaṁ dehe tantur bise yathā
chede bhede sphurad-rūpaṁ cid-brahm-āham-anāmayam

प्रोतांगम् अपि *protāṅgam-api= although pervading*
गुप्तास्यं देहे *guptāsyaṁ dehe =yet remain concealed in body*
तन्तुर्बिसे यथा *tantur bise yathā= like the fibre in stem of water lily flower*
छेदे भेदे स्फुरद् रूपम् *chede bhede sphurad-rūpam= becomes evident upon cutting off or spillting*
चिद्ब्रह्म *cid-brahma= Embodied Brahma*
अहम् अनामयम् *aham-anāmayam= I have become free from afflictions*

This embodied Brahma although pervades all limbs of body, yet it remains concealed (to a person who has failed to realize it), as the fibre in the stem of lotus flower (water lily) though present all over the stem, yet remains concealed. It becomes evident only when the stem is cut off or split. Upon His realization, I have become free from afflictions.

आक्रान्तभुवनाऽप्यभ्रमालेव स्पन्दशालिनी।
दुर्लक्ष्याणुमयाकारा चिच्छक्तिरहमातता।। ८७।।

ākrānt-bhūvanāpyabhra-maleva spandaśālinī
durlakṣy-āṇu-mayākārā cicchaktir-aham-ātatā

आक्रान्तभुवना अपि ākrānt-bhūvanā api=although pervaded the whole universe

अभ्रमाला इव स्पन्दशालिनी *abhra-maleva spandaśālinī=like moving chain of clouds*

दुर्लक्ष्य अणुमयाकारा durlakṣy-āṇu-mayākārā=invisible and atomic in form

चित् शक्तिर् *cit śaktir=embodied Brahma (Energy)*

अहम् आतता *aham-ātatā= I have found it*

Although embodied Brahma (energy) has pervaded the whole universe, as the chain of moving clouds pervades the sky. Yet, I have found it to be invisible and atomic in form.

अनुभूतिमयान्तस्थस्नेहमात्रोपलक्षिता।
क्षीराद्धृतस्य सत्तेव चिदहं क्षयवर्जिता।। ८८।।

anubhūtimay-antasth-snehamātropalakṣitā
kṣirād-dhṛtasya-satteva cidahaṁ kṣaya-varjitā

अनुभूतिमया *anubhūtimaya=can be realized*

अन्तस्थ *antastha=located inside body*

स्नेहमात्र–उपलक्षिता *sneha-mātra-upalakṣitā=through intense love for it*

क्षीराद् घृतस्य सत्तेव *kṣirād-dhṛtasya-satteva=like ghee (clarified butter) in the milk*
चिद् अहम् *cid aham= embodied inner being*
क्षयवर्जिता *kṣaya-varjitā=imperishable*

Embodied inner being is located inside the body and can be realized through intense love for it. It is imperishable and present in the body like ghee (clarified butter) in the milk.

कटकांगदकेयूररचना तदतन्मयी।
हेम्नीव संस्थिता देहे चिद्ब्रह्मात्मास्मि सर्वगः।। ८६।।

kaṭakāṅgad-keyūra-racanā tad-atanmayī
hemnīva sansthitā dehe cidbrahmātmāsmi sarvagḥ

कटक–अंगद–केयूर–रचना *kaṭaka-aṅgad-keyūra-racanā= armlets and bracelets*
तदतन्मयी *tad-atanmayī= have the same form as that of their source material*
हेम्नीव संस्थिता देहे *hemnīva sansthitā dehe= as the gold is pervading their bodies*
चिद्ब्रह्म आत्मास्मि सर्वगः *cidbrahmātmāsmi sarvagḥ= similarly embodied Brahma is pervading our bodies*

As armlets and bracelets being made of gold, have the same form as that of gold. Similarly, Ātmā of our body, being the part of embodied Brahma, has the same form as that of all pervading embodied Brahma.

पदार्थौघस्य शैलादेर्बहिरन्तश्च सर्वदा।
सत्ता सामान्यरूपेण या चित्सोऽहमलेपकः।। ६०।।

padārthaughasya śailāder bahir-antaś ca sarvadā
sattā sāmānya-rūpeṇa yā cit-so'ham-alepakaḥ

पदार्थौघस्य *padārthaughasya=material bodies*
शैलादेर् *śailāder= mountains*
बहिरन्तश्च सर्वदा *bahir-antaś ca sarvadā=pervading as well as invading*
सत्ता सामान्यरूपेण या चित् स: *sattā sāmānya-rūpeṇa yā cit-saḥ = embodied Brahma is common cause of existence*
अहम् अलेपक: *aham-alepakaḥ= I have realized in the state of unmodified awareness (awareness arising from mind being turned to Ātmā)*

This embodied Brahma is also pervading as well as invading the material bodies like mountains. I have realized in the state of unmodified awareness that He is common cause of existence for both living and non living beings.

सर्वासामनुभूतिनामादर्शो यो ह्यकृत्रिमः ।।
अगम्यो मललेखानां तच्चित्तत्वमहं महत् ।। ६१ ।।

sarvāsām-anubhūtinām-ādarśaḥ-yaḥ hi-akṛtrimaḥ
agamyo mala-lekhānāṁ taccittatvam-ahaṁ mahat

सर्वासाम् अनुभूतिनाम् *sarvāsām-anubhūtinām= of all what we have gained or registered as Sanskāras*
आदर्श: य: हि अकृत्रिम: *ādarśaḥ hi-akṛtrimaḥ= that which is natural mirror*
अगम्य: मललेखानाम् *agamyo mala-lekhānāṁ=cannot be explained by layman's writings*
तत् चित् तत्वम् *tat citta-tvam= that is element of unmodified awareness (arising from mind being turned to Ātmā).*
अहं महत् *ahaṁ mahat= It arise due to contact of mind with embodied Ātmā.*

Unmodified awareness is natural mirror reflecting all what we have gained/registered as Sanskāras in our lives. It cannot be explained by a lay man's writings. It arise due to contact of mind with embodied *Ātmā.*

सर्वसंकल्पफलदं सर्वतेजः प्रकाशकम् ।
सर्वोपादेयसीमान्तं चिदात्मानमुपास्महे ।। ६२ ।।

sarvasaṁkalpa-phaladaṁ sarva-tejaḥ prakāśakam
sarvopādeya-sīmāntaṁ cid-ātmānam-upāsmahe

सर्वसंकल्प–फलदम् *arvasaṁkalpa-phaladam= fulfills all willed desires*
सर्वतेजः प्रकाशकम् *sarva-tejaḥ prakāśakam=* illuminator of all illuminating things
सर्व–उपादेय–सीमान्तम् *sarvopādeya-sīmāntam= optimal limit of all useful things*
चिदात्मानम् उपास्महे *cid-ātmānam-upāsmahe= Let us meditate upon embodied Brahma*

Let us meditate upon embodied Brahma. He fulfills all willed desires. He is the illuminator of all illuminating things. He is like the optimal limit of all useful things in the world.

सर्वावयवविश्रान्तं समस्तावयवातिगम् ।
अनारतकचद्रूपं चिदात्मानमुपास्महे ।। ६३ ।।

sarvāvayava-viśrāntaṁ samastāvay-ātigam
anārata-kacd-rūpaṁ cidātmānam-upāsmahe

सर्व–अवयव–विश्रान्तम् *sarvāvayava-viśrāntaṁ= All constituents of creation rest in Him*
समस्त–अवयव–अतिगम् *samastāvay-ātigam= He is above all*
अनारत–कचद्–रुपं *anārata-kacd-rūpam = He illumins continuously*
चिदात्मानम् उपास्महे *cidātmānam-upāsmahe= Let us meditate upon embodied Brahma*

Let us meditate upon embodied Brahma. All constituents of creation rest in Him and He is above all. He illumins continuously.

घटे पटे तटे कूपे स्पन्दमानं सदा तनौ।
जाग्रत्यपि सुषुप्तस्थं चिदात्मानमुपास्महे।। ६४।।

ghaṭe paṭe taṭe kūpe spandamānaṁ sadā tanau
jāgratyapi suṣuptasthaṁ cid-ātmānam upāsmahe

घटे पटे तटे कूपे *ghaṭe paṭe taṭe kūpe= in pot, cloth, river bank or sea shore and a pit well.*
स्पन्दमानं सदा तनौ *spandamānaṁ sadā tanau= He continues to pulsate in non-living bodies and living beings*
जाग्रति अपि सुषुप्तस्थम् *jāgrati api suṣuptasthaṁ= His seeker remains in deep sleep even while awake*
चिदात्मानम् उपास्महे *cid-ātmānam upāsmahe= Let us meditate upon embodied Brahma*

Let us meditate upon embodied Brahma. He is present in pot, cloth, river bank or sea shore and a pit well. He continues to pulsate in non-living bodies and living beings. His seeker remains in deep sleep even while awake.

उष्णमग्नौ हिमे शीतं मृष्टमन्ने शितं क्षुरे।
कृष्णं ध्वान्ते सितं चन्द्रे चिदात्मानमुपास्महे।। ६५।।

uṣṇam-agnau hime śītaṁ mṛṣṭam anne śitaṁ kṣure
kṛṣṇaṁ dhvānte sitaṁ candre cid-ātmānam-upāsmahe

उष्णम् अग्नौ *uṣṇam-agnau= hotness in heat/fire*
हिमे शीतम् *hime śītaṁ=coldness in ice*
मृष्टम् अन्ने *mṛṣṭam anne=sweetness in grain*
शितं क्षुरे *śitaṁ kṣure=sharpness in rajor/sword*
कृष्णं ध्वान्ते *kṛṣṇaṁ dhvānte=blackness in darkness*

सितं चन्द्रे *sitaṁ candre=whiteness in moon*

चिदात्मानम् उपास्महे *cid-ātmānam-upāsmahe= Let us meditate upon embodied Brahma*

Let us meditate upon embodied Brahma. He resides as hotness in heat/fire, coldness in ice, sweetness in grain, sharpness in rajor or sword. He is blackness in darkness, and whiteness in moon.

आलोकं बहिरन्तस्थं स्थितं च स्वात्मवस्तुनि ।
अदूरमपि दूरस्थं चिदात्मानमुपास्महे ।। ६६ ।।

ālokaṁ bahir antasthaṁ sthitaṁ ca svātma-vastuni
adūram api dūrasthaṁ cidātmānam upāsmahe

आलोकं बहिर् अन्तस्थम् *ālokaṁ bahir antasthaṁ= out side as well as inside luster*

स्थितं च स्वात्मवस्तुनि *sthitaṁ ca svātma-vastuni=*. He exists in objects as their Ātmā

अदूरमपि दूरस्थम् *adūram api dūrastham= Although He is located closest (in the heart), yet appears farthest for those who are ignorant of Him*

चिदात्मानम् उपास्महे *cidātmānam upāsmahe=Let us mediate upon embodied Brahma*

Let us meditate upon embodied Brahma. He is out side as well as inside luster. He exists in objects as their Ātmā. Although He is located closest (in the heart), yet appears farthest for those who are ignorant of Him.

माधुर्यादिषु माधुर्यं तीक्ष्णादिषु च तीक्ष्णताम् ।
गतं पदार्थजातेषु चिदात्मानमुपास्महे ।। ६७ ।।

mādhuryādiṣu mādhuryaṁ tīkṣṇādiṣu ca tīkṣṇatām
gataṁ padārthajāteṣu cid-ātmānam-upāsmahe

माधुर्यादिषु माधुर्यं *mādhuryādiṣu mādhuryam= sweetness in sweet things*
तीक्ष्णादिषु च तीक्ष्णताम् *tīkṣṇādiṣu ca tīkṣṇatām=pungentness in pungent things*
गतं पदार्थजातेषु *gataṁ padārthajāteṣu=entered in objects/things as their essence*
चिदात्मानम् उपास्महे *cid-ātmānam-upāsmahe=let us meditate upon embodied Brahma*

Let us meditate upon embodied Brahma. He is sweetness in sweet things like sugar and pungentness in pungent things like chillies. He has entered in objects/things as their essence.

जाग्रत्स्वप्नसुषुप्तेषु तुर्यातुर्यातिगे पदे।
समं सदैव सर्वत्र चिदात्मानमुपास्महे।। ६८।।

jāgrat-svapna-suṣupteṣu turyāturyātige pade
samaṁ sadaiva sarvatra cidātmānam upāsmahe

जाग्रत् –स्वप्न–सुषुप्तेषु *jāgrat-svapna-suṣupteṣu= in all states of awakening, sleep, dream*
तुर्य–अतुर्य–अतिगे पदे *turya-aturya-atige pade= turya, non-turya and beyond turya. Turya means savikalpa samādhi (meditation state). State of awake, sleep and dream are non-turya states. Nirvikalpa samādhi (transcendental meditation state) is the state beyond turya*
समं सदैव सर्वत्र *samaṁ sadaiva sarvatra=undisturbed always in all states*
चिदात्मानम् उपास्महे *cidātmānam upāsmahe=Let us meditate upon embodied Brahma*

Let us meditate upon embodied Brahma. He remains always undistrubed in all states of awakening, sleep, dream, which are known as non-turya, turya, and beyond turya.

प्रशान्तसर्वसंकल्पं विगताखिलकौतुकम्।

विगताशेषसंरम्भं चिदात्मानमुपास्महे।। ९९।।

praśānta-sarva-sankalpaṁ vigat-ākhilakautukam
vigat-aśeṣasanrambhaṁ cid-ātmānam-upāsmahe

प्रशान्त–सर्वसंकल्पम् *praśānta-sarva-sankalpam= all desires are satiated*
विगत–अखिलकौतुकम् *vigat-ākhilakautukam= all curiosities are satisfied*
विगत–अशेषसंरम्भम् *vigat-aśeṣasanrambham= all furies and flurries are gone*
चिदात्मानम् उपास्महे *cid-ātmānam-upāsmahe=Let us meditate upon embodied Brahma*

Let us meditate upon embodied Brahma wherein all desires are satiated, all curiosities are satisfied, all furies and flurries are gone.

निष्कौतुकं निरारम्भं निरीहं सर्वमेव च।
निरंशं निरंहकारं चिदात्मानमुपास्महे।। १००।।

niṣ-kautukam nirārambhaṁ nirīhaṁ sarvam-eva ca
niraṁśaṁ nir-ahaṅkāraṁ cid-ātmānam upāsmahe

निष्कौतुकम् *niṣ-kautukam=free from curiosity*
निर् आरम्भम् *nir-ārambham= free from undertaking enterprise*
निर् ईहम् *nir-īham= free from desires*
सर्वम् एव च *sarvam-eva ca= all*
निर् अंशम् *nir-aṁśam=stakes/shares*
निर् अंहकारम् *nir-ahaṅkāram=egotism*
चिदात्मानम् उपास्महे *cid-ātmānam upāsmahe=Let us meditate upon embodied Brahma*

Let us meditate upon embodied Brahma. He will make us free from all curiosities, undertaking enterprises, desires, stakes or shares, and egotism.

सर्वस्यान्तः स्थितं सर्वमप्यपारैकरूपिणम् ।
अपर्यन्तचिदारम्भं चिदात्मानमुपागतः ।। १०१ ।।

sarvasy-āntaḥ sthitaṁ sarvam-apyapāraikarupiṇam
aparyanta-cidārambhaṁ cidātmānam upāgataḥ

सर्वस्यान्तः स्थितम् *sarvasya-antaḥ sthitam=established inside all*
सर्वम् अपि अपार–एकरूपिणम् *sarvam-api-apāra-ekarupiṇam =unbounded by all and remains unchanged*
अपर्यन्तचिद् आरम्भम् *aparyanta-cid-ārambham=cause of manifestation of limitless Individuated Ātmā-s (Ātmā-s manifesting in the form of various living beings)*
चिदात्मानम् उपागतः *cid-ātmānam upāgataḥ=Meditate upon embodied Brahma*

Meditate upon Embodied Brahma. He is established inside all, yet unbounded by all and remains unchanged. He is the cause of manifestation of limitless individuated Ātmā-s.

त्रैलोक्यदेहमुक्तानां तन्तुमुन्नतमाततम् ।
प्रचारसंकोचकरं चिदात्मानमुपागतः ।। १०२ ।।

trailokya-deha-muktānāṁ tantum-unnatam-ātatam
pracāra-saṅkocakaraṁ cidātmānam upāgataḥ

त्रैलोक्य–देहमुक्तानाम् *railokya-deha-muktānām=beads of bodies existing in the three lokas*
तन्तुम् उन्नतम् आततम् *tantum-unnatam-ātatam=sublime thread strung although*
प्रचार–संकोचकरम् *pracāra-saṅkocakaram=capable of making expansion and contraction*
चिदात्मानम् उपागतः *cid-ātmānam upāgataḥ=Meditate upon embodied Brahma*

Meditate upon embodied Brahma. He is a sublime thread strung although all beads of bodies existing in the three lokas. He is capable of making expansion and contraction.

लीनमन्तर्बहिः स्वाप्तान्क्रोडीकृत्यजगत्खगान् ।
चित्रं बृहज्जालमिव चिदात्मानमुपागतः ।। १०३ ।।

līnam-antar-bahiḥ svāptān-kroḍī-kṛtya-jagat-khagān
citraṁ bṛhajjālamiva cid-ātmānam-upāgataḥ

लीनम् अन्तर् बहिः *līnam-antar-bahiḥ=hidden inside and outside*
स्वाप्तान् *svāptān=abundant*
क्रोडीकृत्य *kroḍī-kṛtya=having gathered*
जगत्खगान् *jagat-khagān=planets and stars*
चित्रम् *citraṁ=vivacious*
बृहज्जालम् इव *bṛhajjālam iva= like a huge network of stars*
चिदात्मानम् उपागतः *cid-ātmānam-upāgataḥ=meditate upon embodied Brahma*

Meditate upon embodied Brahma. He, having gathered abundant planets and stars, is hidden inside and outside of all. He is vivacious like a huge network of stars.

सर्वं यत्रेदमस्त्येव नास्त्येव च मनागपि ।
सदसद्रूपमेकं तं चिदात्मानमुपागतः ।। १०४ ।।

sarvaṁ yatredam astyeva nāstyeva ca manāgapi
sad-asad-rūpam-ekaṁ taṁ cid-ātmānam upāgataḥ

सर्वम् *sarvam=All things*
यत्र *yatra=in whom*
इदम् अस्ति एव *edam astyeva=this world exists during creation*
न अस्ति एव च मनाक् अपि *nāstyeva ca manāgapi= nothing (not even a single thing) exist during dissolution*

सद्–असद् रूपम् *sad-asad-rūpam=both imperishable and perishable*
एकं तम् *ekaṁ tam=unique*
चिदात्मानम् उपागतः *cid-ātmānam upāgataḥ=Meditate upon embodied Brahma*

Meditate upon embodied Brahma, in whom exists this universe during creation and nothing exists during dissolution. As such, He is both *sadrūpa* (Himself being imperishable) and *asadrūpa* (His creation being perishable)

परमप्रत्ययं पूर्णमास्पदं सर्वसंपदाम्।
सर्वाकारविहारस्थं चिदात्मानमुपागतः।। १०५।।

param-pratyayaṁ pūrṇam-āspadaṁ sarva-saṁpadām
sarvākāra-vihārasthaṁ cid-ātmānam upāgataḥ

परमप्रत्ययम् *param-pratyayam=most trusted*
पूर्णम् आस्पदम् *pūrṇam-āspadam=complete seat*
सर्वसंपदाम् *sarva-saṁpadām=all fortunes*
सर्व–आकार–विहारस्थम् *sarva-ākāra-vihārastham= exists in all types of bodies and places*
चिदात्मानम् उपागतः *cid-ātmānam upāgataḥ=meditate upon embodied Brahma*

Meditate upon embodied Brahma. He is most trusted and a complete seat of all fortunes. He exists in all types of bodies and places.

स्नेहाधारमथोऽशान्तं जडवाताहतिभ्रमैः।
युक्तं मुक्तं च चिद्दीपं बहिरन्तरुपास्महे।। १०६।।

sneh-ādhāram-atho'śāntaṁ jaḍ-vātāhati-bhramaiḥ
yuktaṁ muktaṁ ca ciddīpaṁ bahir-antar-upāsmahe

स्नेहाधारम् *sneh-ādhāram= burning with the help of oil, for fondness or affection to Brahma*
अथ अशान्तम् *atha aśāntam= disturb*
जडवात–आहतिभ्रमैः *jaḍa-vāta-āhati-bhramaiḥ=whirlpool evolved from motionless winds*
युक्तम् *yuktam= bondage of Ātmā with physical body*
मुक्तं च *muktaṁ ca= free*
चिद् दीपम् *cid-dīpam=lamp of embodied Ātmā*
बहिर् अन्तर् *bahir-antar=from outside and inside*
उपास्महे *upāsmahe= Let us meditate upon the embodied Brahma*

Let us meditate upon the Brahma, so that the flames of lamp of embodied Ātmā, burning for fondness or affection to Brahma, remains free from disturbance of its bondage with physical body from outside, and vital air from inside, as the whirlpool evolved from the motionless wind is unable to disturb the flame of lamp (burning with the help of oil).

हृत्सरः पद्मिनीकन्दं तन्तुं सर्वांगसुन्दरम्।
जनताजीवनोपायं चिदात्मानमुपागतः।। १०७।।

hṛtsaraḥ padminīkandaṁ tantuṁ sarvāṅg-sundaram
janatājīvanopāyaṁ cidātmānam upāgataḥ

हृत्सरः *hṛtsaraḥ= pond of heart*
पद्मिनीकन्दम् *padminīkandaṁ=root of lotus flower*
तन्तुम् *tantuṁ=string*
सर्वांग–सुन्दरम् *sarvāṅga-sundaram=beautiful by all means*
जनताजीवनोपायम् *janatājīvanopāyaṁ=means of life*
चिदात्मानमुपागतः *cidātmānam upāgataḥ= meditate upon embodied Brahma*

Disclosing the abode of Ātmā in the body, Vasiṣṭha says: Meditate upon embodied Brahma. He has His roots in the heart in the form of Ātmā, like the lotus flower in pond. He is a beautiful string which is the means of life of all living beings.

अक्षीरार्णवसंभूतमशशांकमुपस्थितम् ।
अहार्यममृतं सत्यं चिदात्मानमुपास्महे ।। १०८ ।।

akṣīrārṇava-saṁbhūtam-aśaśāṅkam upasthitam
ahāryam-amṛtaṁ satyaṁ cid-ātmānam upāsmahe

अक्षीर–अर्णव–संभूतम् *akṣīr-ārṇava-saṁbhūtam=not born of kṣīra sāgara (space) (pauranic allegory of churning of ocean where space symbolizes kṣīra sāgara (white ocean), churning symbolizes rotation of earth about its axis)*
अशशांकम् उपस्थितम् *aśaśāṅkam upasthitam= not present in moon*
अहार्यम् *ahāryam = not stolen by Garuḍa (paurāṇika allegory depicting light as amṛta, celestial sphere as the abode of light (amṛta) and sun as Garuḍa (vehicle of light)*
अमृतम् *amṛtam=nectre*
सत्यम् *satyam=eternal*
चिदात्मानम् उपास्महे *cid-ātmānam upāsmahe=let us meditate upon embodied Brahma*

Let us meditate upon embodied Brahma, an eternal nectre which is not born of kṣīra sāgara during churning of ocean, neither is present in moon, nor is stolen by Garuḍa.

शब्दरूपरसस्पर्शगन्धैराभासमागतम् ।
तैरेव रहितं शान्तं चिदात्मानमुपागतः ।। १०९ ।।

śabdarūpa-rasa-sparśa-gandhair-ābhāsam-āgatam
taireva rahitaṁ śāntaṁ cid-ātmānam-upāgataḥ

शब्द–रूप–रस–स्पर्श–गन्धैर् *śabdarūpa-rasa-sparśa-gandhair= by the elementary sensations of sound, sight, taste, touch and* *smell*

आभासम् आगतम् *ābhāsam-āgatam=is manifested*

तैरेव रहितम् *taireva rahitaṁ=without which*

शान्तम् *śāntam= it remains unmanifest*

चिदात्मानम् उपागतः *cid-ātmānam-upāgataḥ=meditate upon embodied Brahma*

Meditate upon embodied Brahma, Who is manifested by elementary sensations of sound, sight, taste, touch and smell, without which He remains unmanifest.

आकाशकोशविशदं सर्वलोकस्य रंजनम्।
न रंजनं न चाकाशं चिदात्मानमुपागतः। ११०।।

ākāśa-kośa-viśadaṁ sarvaloksya rañjanam
na rañjanaṁ na cākāśaṁ cid-ātmānam upāgataḥ

आकाश–कोश–विशदम् *ākāśa-kośa-viśadam= as vast and extended as the expansive network of sky*

सर्वलोकस्य रंजनम् *sarvaloksya rañjanam=makes all worlds visible*

न रंजनम् *na rañjanam= Himself neither visible*

न च आकाशम् *na cākāśam= nor expansive like sky*

चिदात्मानम् उपागतः *cid-ātmānam upāgataḥ=meditate upon embodied Brahma*

Meditate upon embodied Brahma. He is as vast and extended as the expansive netork of sky and makes all worlds visible, but He Himself is neither visible nor expansive like sky.

महामहिम्ना सहितं रहितं सर्वभूतिभिः।
कर्तृत्वे वाप्यकर्तारं चिदात्मानमुपागतः।। १११।।

mahā-mahimnā sahitaṁ rahitaṁ sarvabhūtibhiḥ
kartṛtve vāpyakartāraṁ cid-ātmānam upāgataḥ

महामहिम्ना सहितम् *mahā-mahimnā sahitam= endowed with all power and fortune*
रहितं सर्वभूतिभिः *rahitaṁ sarva-bhūtibhiḥ= doesn't enjoy all fortunes*
कर्तृत्वे वा अपि अकर्तारम् *kartṛtve vāpi akartāram= although he does everyting, but not the doer*
चिदात्मानम् उपागतः *cid-ātmānam upāgataḥ=meditate upon embodied Brahma*

Meditate upon embodied Brahma. He is endowed with all power and fortunes, but never enjoys them. Though He does everything, but nevertheless a doer.

अखिलमिदमहं ममैव सर्वं त्वहमपि नाहमथेतरच्च नाहम्।
इति विदितवतो जगत्कृतं मे स्थिरमथवास्तु गतज्वरो भवामि।।
११२।।

akhilam-idam-ahaṁ mamaiva sarvaṁ tvaham-api nāham-athetaracca nāham iti viditvato jagat-kṛtaṁ me sthiram-athavāstu gatajvaro bhavāmi

अखिलम् इदम् अहम् *akhilam-idam-ahaṁ= This all is born of embodied Brahma*
ममैव सर्वं तु *mamaiva sarvaṁ tu=as everyting belongs to Him*
अहम् अपि न अहम् *aham-api nāham= I don't have my separate existence independent of Brahma*
अथ इतरत् च न अहम् *atha itarat ca na aham= other things are not dependant upon me, but on Brahma*
इति विदितवतः *iti viditvato=having realized it*
जगत्कृतं मे स्थिरम् *jagat-kṛtaṁ me sthiram=my view about world*
अथवा अस्तु *athavā astu=has changed*
गतज्वरः भवामि *gata-jvaraḥ bhavāmi= and my fever of illusion is over*

This all is born of embodied Brahma, as everything belongs to Him. Even I don't have my separate existence independent of Brahma. Other things are not dependant upon me either. Having realized it, my view about world has changed and my fever of illusion is over.

इत्यार्षे श्रीवसिष्ठमहारामायणे वाल्मीकीये मोक्षोपाये निर्वाणप्रकरणे जीवन्मुक्तनिश्चययोगोपदेशो नाम एकादशः सर्गः।

This is the end of the Eleventh Chapter on 'Liberated Life' of Yoga Vāsiṣṭha Mahārāmāyaṇa, known as Mokṣopāya, Authored by Guru Maharishi Vālmīki.

Glossary of Technical Terms in *Yogavāsiṣṭha*

1. Satya: Satya is that which exists always and remains unchanged. Brahma is Satya
2. Mithyā: Mithyā is that which comes into existence for a short while and is ever changing. This world Jagat is mithyā. Mithyā objects or things cannot give us lasting happiness. Only Satya can give us lasting happiness.
3. Karma: willful or intentional action is called karma. There are several functions that body performs, such as breathing, blood circulation and the rest, but these do not tmqualify as actions, as there is no intention or will behind them. Similarly unintended acions by humans cannot be called actions. Only intentional actions that are guided by manas, buddhi and ahankara are subject to blame and praise. Going by this logic, when we become give up ahankara and control mental faculties and begin according to ṛta (inner law), we become free from pāpa and puṇya.
4. Pāpa : immoral or unethical karmas
5. Puṇya: Moral and ethical karmas
6. Ṛta: Inner Law
7. Manas: ability to think, desire and imagin
8. Buddhi: ability to make decisions or arrive at conclusions
9. Ahaṅkāra: ability to maintain distinct individual identity
10. Citta: mind based awareness, when mind is turned towards external senses. It is a form of bio-electric current in a living body which sends messages to brain as its centre. It is a link between manas and spanda (prāṇa vāyu). Both manas and prāṇa are interlinked with the help of citta. If we are able to control manas, we can have a

control over prāṇa. If we control prāṇa, can have a control over manas.

11. Cid Aham: ahaṁkārita (embodied) Ātmā
12. Cit/Cid: unmodified awareness when mind is turned within.
13. Spanda: Prāṇa vāyu (breathings)
14. Ātmā : Individuated Ātmā. Also called as Puruṣa.
15. Cid Ātmā: embodied Brahma
16. Aham: Ātmā
17. Jñāna: Enlightenment
18. Jñānī: Enlightened
19. Ajñāna: ignorance/absence of information
20. Ajñānī: Uninformed/ignorant
21. Ātmajñāna: Realization of Ātmā
22. Paraṁ Brahma: Absolute Supreme Paramātmā that exists even beyond universal creation.
23. Cid Brahma: embodied Brahma (Paramātmā) pervading an animate or inanimate body whther it is small of big like our universe. Also called as Brahmāṇda Puruṣa, Brahmāṇḍa Cetanā or Indra. Its physical property is electric current prevalent in the entire universe.
24. Brahma: pure Paramātmā
25. Brahma-jñāna: Realization of Paramātmā.
26. Māyā: Matter and material objects.

www.ingramcontent.com/pod-product-compliance
Lightning Source LLC
Chambersburg PA
CBHW060404050426
42449CB00009B/1898
* 9 7 8 8 1 8 7 7 1 0 8 3 7 *